TARUN TAKSHAY

Middle Class Trap To Millionaire Mindset

How to Unlock the Millionaire Mindset and Multiply Your Income

TAKSHAY
DIGITAL ACADEMY

First published by Takshay Digital Academy 2025

First edition

ISBN: 978-93-344-4276-2

This book was professionally typeset on Reedsy.
Find out more at reedsy.com

To every dreamer who feels stuck in the 9–5 jobs and feeling Trap in middle class, who hesitates to take risks, yet yearns for freedom—this book is for you.

To My Beloved Lord Krishna,
The source of my inspiration, wisdom, and courage.
Every word in this book is not mine alone—it is guided by Your grace. Just as You held Arjuna's chariot and illuminated his path with truth, You have held my heart and guided me on this journey of creation.

This book is my humble offering at Your lotus feet.

"The middle-class mindset builds comfort.
The millionaire mindset builds freedom.
Which one will you choose?"

"Your current life is the result of your past thoughts.
Your future life will be the result of the thoughts you choose today."

"The trap is not your job, your salary, or your bank balance.
The real trap is your belief about what's possible."

— Tarun Takshay

Contents

Foreword

We live in a world where millions of people work tirelessly every single day, yet only a few ever break free from the endless cycle of bills, stress, and the 9-to-5 routine. For most, the "middle-class dream" of a steady job, a house, and security slowly turns into a trap — leaving little room for real freedom.

This book is a wake-up call. It's not just about money; it's about **mindset**. The author challenges the traditional beliefs that many of us have grown up with — the idea that hard work alone guarantees success, that saving is the only path to wealth, and that playing safe is better than taking risks.

What you're about to read will shake the way you think. It will help you see opportunities where others see obstacles, and it will show you how an ordinary person with the right mindset can create extraordinary results.

If you have ever felt stuck in your career, trapped by financial limitations, or uncertain about how to take control of your future, this book will give you the clarity and courage you need.

Read these pages with an open mind. Let the ideas challenge you, inspire you, and most importantly, move you to take action. Because the truth is — financial freedom doesn't start in your wallet. It starts in your mind.

Tarun Takshay
Takshay Digital Academy

Preface

Most middle-class people live by an unspoken script: school → college → job → retirement. They follow the path of "safety," thinking it guarantees stability, yet it rarely leads to financial freedom.

This book challenges that mindset. It shows you:

- How to **break limiting beliefs** holding you back.
- How to **start a side hustle** that grows over time.
- How to **manage money, reinvest profits, and create small wins** that build confidence.
- How to **scale these wins into sustainable income and financial independence**.

Each chapter is written in a **story-driven, simple style**, with exercises and actionable steps. It's designed for people **who want freedom but don't know where to start**.

Think of this book as your **companion guide, mentor, and daily motivator**. By the time you finish, you will have a **practical roadmap**, not just theory—a plan to move from comfort and fear to **confidence, action, and financial growth**.

Welcome to your journey. It starts here.

Every great success story starts with a decision — the decision to no longer settle.

This book, *Middle-Class Trap to Millionaire Mindset,* is not just another self-help guide. It is your **wake-up call**. A declaration that you are destined for more than just paying bills, living in fear, and waiting for retirement to enjoy life.

The world doesn't reward hard work alone. It rewards courage. It rewards vision. It rewards those who dare to think differently.

- The middle-class mindset asks: *"Is this safe?"*
- The millionaire mindset asks: *"Is this worth it?"*
- The middle-class mindset says: *"I'll do it when I have more time."*
- The millionaire mindset says: *"I'll create the time, because this matters."*
- The middle-class mindset lives for weekends.
- The millionaire mindset designs a life that doesn't need escape.

This book exists to **shift your thinking instantly**. From the very first chapter, you won't be told what's wrong with your life — you'll be shown how to unlock what's possible.

You don't need permission. You don't need to wait. You don't even need to know all the steps yet. What you need is a **mindset shift**. And once that happens, everything else — money, opportunities, freedom — will follow.

Let this book be your spark. Because once your mindset changes, nothing can stop you.

Prologue

I still remember sitting at my desk — trapped in the same routine, staring at the clock, and wondering if life was meant to be just this. Deep inside, I dreamed of financial freedom, of breaking out of the cycle of working for survival instead of living with purpose. But I didn't know where to start.

Like many of you, I asked myself:

- *How do I escape the middle-class trap that keeps me limited?*
- *Is it really possible to start a side hustle and turn it into something life-changing?*
- *Can I build the confidence, habits, and mindset that attract wealth and freedom?*

This book is my answer. It is written for dreamers stuck in a 9-to-5, for freelancers searching for growth, for students ready to build something bigger, and for every person who feels the fire inside but hasn't yet found the path.

Here, I've distilled not just my personal journey, but also the inspiring stories of ordinary people who dared to take extraordinary steps. Inside, you'll discover practical exercises, powerful strategies, and mindset shifts designed to move you from limitation to liberation.

I promise not to bury you in complex theories or business jargon. Instead, I'll guide you with simple, actionable steps — the kind you can apply immediately. Because it's not giant leaps but small, consistent actions that create unstoppable momentum toward financial freedom.

My mission is clear: to help you unlock a millionaire mindset, break free from the invisible walls holding you back, and design a life of confidence, wealth, and freedom — one bold step at a time.

— **Tarun Takshay**

Introduction

Most of us grow up with the same script:

Go to school. Get good grades. Find a stable job. Work hard. Save for retirement.

It sounds safe. It sounds responsible. It even sounds like success.

But if you look closer, you'll see the hidden trap — a routine that keeps millions of people stuck in the same cycle, year after year. Work. Earn. Spend. Repeat.

This is what I call the middle-class trap.

The middle class often lives with just enough to feel comfortable, but not enough to feel free. You may have a steady income, but you also have debts, bills, and responsibilities that tie you down. You may feel secure today, but deep down you know that one economic shift, one job loss, or one health crisis could change everything.

I wrote this book because I have lived through that cycle — and I know there's a way out. The difference between staying stuck and breaking free isn't luck, inheritance, or secret shortcuts. It's **mindset**.

The way millionaires think, decide, and act is fundamentally different from the middle-class mindset. While most people trade time for money, millionaires create systems that make money work for them. While most people avoid risks, millionaires calculate and embrace them. While most people focus on survival, millionaires focus on growth.

This book is not about overnight riches. It's not about quick fixes or unrealistic promises. Instead, it's a roadmap to **shift your thinking** — to help you recognize the beliefs and habits that keep you trapped, and replace them with the mindset that leads to financial freedom.

As you go through these chapters, I want you to imagine a life beyond the 9-to-5 routine — a life where money is not a constant source of stress, but a tool that supports your dreams. A life where you choose how to spend your time, instead of selling it to the highest bidder.

Close your eyes for a moment. Picture your dream life. The freedom to wake up without an alarm clock. The ability to choose where you live, how you spend your time, and who you spend it with. The power to say **yes** to experiences most people only dream of.

Now open your eyes and realize this: it's not fantasy. It's possible. And the only thing standing between you and that life is the way you think.

The middle-class trap is built on fear and limitation. People are told:

- "Play it safe."
- "Don't take risks."
- "Be grateful you even have a job."

But here's the truth: playing it safe is the biggest risk of all. Because safety keeps you average. Safety keeps you small. Safety keeps you trapped.

Millionaires, on the other hand, see the world differently:

- Where others see problems, they see opportunities.

- Where others say, *"I can't,"* they ask, *"How can I?"*
- Where others spend, they invest.
- Where others stop, they persist.

And here's the best part — you don't need to be born rich or lucky to adopt this mindset. It's available to anyone who chooses it.

This book is your guide to making that choice. You'll discover practical ways to break free from limiting beliefs and step into a mindset of power, abundance, and freedom.

Remember: You don't need a miracle. You don't need a lottery ticket. You don't need permission from anyone.

You only need to decide: *Will I continue to think like the masses, or will I rise with the mindset of the few?*

The middle-class trap is powerful, but so is your potential. This book will show you how to unlock it.

Let's begin.

Tarun Takshay
Founder - Takshay Digital Academy

1

Comfortable But Trapped

"H*ave you ever looked around at your life and thought, 'Is this really all there is?'"*

If you're reading this book, chances are you've felt it. Maybe you've followed the script your parents, teachers, or society wrote for you: study hard, get a degree, land a decent 9–5 job, save money, and retire someday. Comfortable, right? Safe, right? But somewhere deep down, a small voice whispers, *"I want more. I want freedom. I want to be financially independent."*

Let me tell you a secret I've learned on my journey: **comfort is the biggest trap of all**. And yes—I've been there. Growing up in a middle-class family, security always felt like the most important thing. Salary was reliable, bills were paid, and life seemed "safe." But that comfort kept me from dreaming bigger. It kept me small while I secretly wished to join the 100 Cr club someday.

The Hidden Cost of Comfort

Comfort isn't just about money. It's about mindset. When you're too comfortable, you stop taking risks, trying new things, and exploring opportunities. You stick to what feels safe. And here's the problem: **wealth rarely grows in your comfort zone**.

Think about it: your salary increases slowly, taxes and inflation eat away your savings, and suddenly, even after years of working, you realize that your financial freedom is still years away. That's the middle-class trap.

I remember my first "realization moment." I was earning a decent salary, had a small apartment, and even a car loan I was proud of. Life seemed perfect. But one day, I saw someone my age—someone who had started a small side hustle—making more in a month than I earned in three. That shook me. It made me realize: **comfort had lulled me into believing I was on the path to success, when in reality, I was just surviving.**

Reflection Exercise:

Take a moment. Write down **three areas in your life where you feel too comfortable**. Is it your job? Your spending habits? Your fear of trying something new? Awareness is the first step to breaking free.

Comfort = Risk Aversion

Most people think they are avoiding risk by staying comfortable. But here's the truth: **not taking risks is the biggest risk of all**. The longer you wait, the harder it becomes to start, and the more opportunities pass you by.

Imagine this: 10 years from now, you're still in the same job, your salary might have grown, but your dreams of financial freedom are still just dreams. Now imagine taking just one small step today—a side hustle, a new skill, an investment—and watching your life slowly shift. Which version of you do you want to meet in the mirror?

Your First Step Out of the Trap

This book isn't about abandoning stability recklessly. It's about **starting smart, taking calculated risks, and creating a safety net while growing wealth**. In the next chapters, I'll show you how even middle-class people—housewives, freelancers, office-goers—can start building assets, mindset, and habits that multiply wealth.

But it all begins with this: **recognize the trap, feel the discomfort, and commit to change**.

Remember, I've been where you are. I've felt that fear, that hesitation. And I made the decision to start small, learn fast, and grow steadily. If I can do it, so can you.

Actionable Exercise:

1. List the 3 biggest "comfortable zones" in your life.
2. For each, write **one small step** you can take this week to start moving out of that zone.
3. Commit to completing at least one action by Sunday.

2

Why Jobs Alone Won't Make You Rich

"We all grew up believing that a steady job is the key to security. But what if I told you that the very thing you're relying on is actually keeping you from becoming rich?"

I still remember my first job after college. I was thrilled—steady salary, office ID card, perks. Everyone around me applauded my "success." But after a few months, a tiny nagging thought started creeping in: *"Is this enough?"*

The answer? Not really. Let me explain why.

The Income Ceiling

When you rely solely on a job, your income is capped. No matter how hard you work, there's a limit. You get promotions, maybe a bonus, but your earning potential grows **linearly**, not exponentially.

I've seen countless colleagues working 10–12 hours a day, thinking more hours = more money. But here's the harsh reality: time is finite. You can't stretch a day beyond 24 hours, no matter how many projects you take.

Contrast that with entrepreneurs or people who build side hustles: they create systems, products, or services that earn while they sleep. Suddenly, growth becomes **exponential**, not capped by a fixed salary.

Inflation and Lifestyle Creep

Another invisible trap is what I call **"lifestyle creep."** As your salary increases, so do your expenses—better car, bigger apartment, fancy gadgets. Even though you earn more, your net wealth may barely move.

I faced this myself. My first salary jump felt amazing. But within months, I was paying EMIs and upgrading lifestyle items. It felt like running on a treadmill: moving fast but staying in the same place financially.

Jobs Don't Teach Wealth Creation

Here's the biggest problem: jobs teach you **how to be an employee**, not how to be financially free. You learn how to follow instructions, meet deadlines, and manage office politics—but rarely about:

- Creating multiple streams of income
- Investing wisely
- Building systems that work for you

I realized early that if I wanted real wealth, I couldn't just rely on a 9–5. I had to **think like a builder, not just a worker**.

My Wake-Up Call

A friend of mine, let's call him Ramesh, worked at a reputed IT firm. He earned more than many of his peers, lived comfortably, and had all the perks. Yet, one day, he confided:

"I feel stuck. I work hard, but at the end of the month, I'm still not closer to my dreams."

That hit me. And it hit Ramesh too. That conversation sparked his journey into starting a small online business while still working his full-time job. Today, a few years later, he earns more from his side business than his IT job—and has options and freedom he never had before.

Reflection Exercise:

1. Write down your **monthly income vs monthly expenses**. Be honest.
2. Identify 1 area where your salary increases haven't improved your financial freedom.
3. Ask yourself: *"If I keep doing the same thing for 5–10 years, where will I be financially?"*

The Key Takeaway

Relying solely on a job is comfortable—but it's a trap if your goal is financial freedom or becoming a millionaire. Jobs give **security**, but not **wealth**.

The good news? You don't have to quit your job tomorrow. You just need to start building **additional income streams** now—small, smart, manageable steps that eventually compound into real freedom.

Actionable Step for This Week:

- List **one skill or hobby** you can monetize on the side.
- Spend at least **1 hour each day this week** learning or practicing how to turn it into income.
- Remember: small consistent action beats waiting for the "perfect time" to start.

3

The Myth of "Safe Choices"

"We're told to play it safe. Get a degree, get a job, retire comfortably. But what if the very things we're taught to believe are safe are actually keeping us from becoming rich?"

If you've ever wondered why most people never become financially free, this chapter is for you. Let's talk about **the illusion of safety** and how societal conditioning shapes our decisions.

Societal Conditioning: The Middle-Class Script

From a young age, we're taught a simple formula:

1. Study hard.
2. Get a stable job.
3. Buy a house, car, and maybe a small vacation each year.
4. Save for retirement.

Follow these steps and you'll have a "safe life." Sounds good, right? It did to me, growing up in a middle-class household. I remember my parents emphasizing, *"Just get a secure job, that's all you need."*

But here's the truth: this "safe path" rarely leads to wealth. Why? Because it's designed to **minimize risk, not maximize opportunity**. It keeps you inside a comfort zone where earning potential is capped, creativity is restricted, and wealth creation is slow.

Safety Often Feels Comfortable, But It's a Trap

I've lived this. My first few years in a secure job felt great—I had a salary, savings, and recognition. But I noticed something: my dreams of building wealth, achieving freedom, or creating a business that works while I sleep were **stalling**.

Comfort was keeping me trapped. I was earning, but I wasn't growing. I realized that **safe choices feel good short-term but limit long-term growth**.

Examples of "Safe Choices" That Hold People Back

1. **Only studying for grades or a degree** instead of learning real-world skills like sales, marketing, or entrepreneurship.
2. **Working a secure 9–5** and believing salary alone will make you rich.
3. **Avoiding investments or side hustles** because they feel risky.

I know people who followed all these "safe" rules perfectly but still struggled financially. And then there are those who took calculated risks—learning online skills, starting a small business, investing wisely—and eventually gained financial freedom much earlier.

My First Risky Decision

I remember when I first considered starting a small online side hustle while still in my full-time job. It felt risky. Friends and family said, *"Why jeopardize your stable income?"*

I hesitated for weeks. Then I realized: the only real risk is **not trying at all**. That first small step—a simple freelance project—was uncomfortable, but it taught me that **action beats comfort every time**. That single decision began a chain of growth that would eventually lead me toward my millionaire mindset.

Reflection Exercise

Take a pen and paper and write down:

1. Three "safe choices" you are currently holding onto that feel comfortable but may be limiting your growth.
2. For each, ask: *"What's the real risk if I start taking small steps toward change?"*
3. Identify **one small action** you can take this week to challenge at least one "safe choice."

Key Takeaway

Safety is an illusion. Comfort can feel good, but it often masks **missed opportunities**. True financial freedom requires stepping out of the predictable path, learning new skills, taking small calculated risks, and building something that works for you.

Actionable Step for This Week:

- Pick one "safe choice" you are clinging to.
- Take **one small action** toward breaking it: e.g., enroll in a short course, apply for freelance work, or research a potential side hustle.
- Track your progress and reflect at the end of the week.

4

Assets vs Liabilities Made Simple

"It's not how much money you earn, but how much money you keep—and how smartly you make it work for you—that decides whether you become rich."

This is one lesson I learned the hard way. For years, I thought earning a higher salary was the key to wealth. But I noticed something: my salary increased, my lifestyle improved, yet my net worth barely moved. Something was wrong. That's when I discovered the simple but powerful difference between **assets and liabilities**.

What Are Assets and Liabilities?

I'll keep it simple:

- **Assets**: Things that put money **into your pocket**.
- **Liabilities**: Things that **take money out of your pocket**.

Think of it like a river: assets are streams that flow toward you; liabilities are leaks that drain your river. If you want to grow wealth, you need **more streams flowing in than money leaking out**.

Everyday Examples Middle-Class People Can Relate To

Home Loan / Apartment

- Most people think their house is an asset. But if you're paying huge EMIs and it doesn't generate income, it's actually a liability.
- Exception: A rental property that earns more than its cost is an asset.

Car / Vehicle

- Many buy cars on EMIs, thinking it's a status symbol. But it depreciates fast, costs maintenance, fuel, insurance—it's a liability.
- Compare with: Using a car to start a delivery business or rideshare side hustle—then it can become an asset.

Investments / Side Hustles

- Stocks, mutual funds, or a small online business that generates recurring income? That's an asset.

Luxury Items

- Gadgets, branded clothing, or the latest phone: often liabilities, unless used to **create income or business opportunities**.

The Middle-Class Mistake

Most of us spend our lives buying liabilities, thinking they are assets. We're taught: "Buy a house, get a car, save for retirement." But without income-producing assets, **wealth doesn't grow**, no matter how much we earn.

I've seen it in my own life. Early in my career, I bought a car on EMI thinking it was a symbol of success. A few years later, I realized it was draining my income, while my side hustle and small investments were quietly building real wealth. That moment reshaped my mindset entirely.

How to Start Thinking Like a Millionaire

1. **Track your money**: Separate what goes into assets vs. liabilities.
2. **Prioritize income-generating purchases**: Small investments that pay back over time.
3. **Avoid lifestyle inflation traps**: Just because you earn more doesn't mean you must spend more.

Reflection Exercise

1. List **3 liabilities** in your life that are draining your income.
2. For each liability, ask: *"Can I convert this into an asset, or reduce its cost?"*
3. Write **one small action** you can take this week to start turning a liability into an asset.

Example: Instead of spending ₹15,000 on a car EMI, consider using the same amount to invest in a skill that could earn ₹20,000/month or more.

Key Takeaway

Becoming rich isn't about earning more; it's about **building a flow of assets that work for you**, while minimizing liabilities. Start thinking in terms of **streams of income**, not just salary increments. Once you shift this mindset, every rupee you spend can either work for you—or against you.

Actionable Step for This Week:

- Identify **one liability** you can reduce or transform into an income-generating asset.
- Take **one concrete action** to make this change this week.
- Reflect at the end of the week: notice how small adjustments start shifting your mindset.

5

From Earners to Builders / Breaking Limiting Beliefs

"Most people earn money. Few people build wealth. And even fewer understand the mindset required to make that leap."

If you've ever felt stuck in your 9–5, chasing salary increments, bonuses, and yearly appraisals, this chapter is your wake-up call. The difference between a lifelong earner and a builder of wealth isn't luck—it's mindset.

Earners vs Builders: What's the Difference?

Earners:

- Exchange time for money.
- Rely on jobs, salaries, and limited income streams.
- Seek comfort, avoiding risk.

Builders:

- Create systems that earn while they sleep.
- Build multiple income streams.
- Take calculated risks, learn fast, and iterate.

I used to be an earner. For years, I believed a higher salary was success. Then I met a few entrepreneurs and side-hustlers who were my age, some even younger, quietly building multiple streams of income. They weren't taking reckless risks—they were **acting smartly, consistently, and boldly**.

That's when I realized: being comfortable as an earner is easy. But **to become rich, you need to build**.

Breaking Limiting Beliefs

Most of us are unknowingly trapped by beliefs like:

- "I need a degree to be successful."
- "Risk is dangerous, better stay safe."
- "I don't have enough money or skills to start."

These beliefs silently dictate our life choices, keeping us small while dreams of wealth feel distant.

Here's a personal story:

When I first considered starting a side hustle, I was paralyzed by fear. "What if I fail?" I asked myself. "What if people judge me?" I realized I was letting **limiting beliefs define my potential**.

So, I started small. One freelance project, one investment, one learning opportunity at a time. Each small success chipped away at those limiting beliefs. Soon, fear transformed into curiosity, doubt into experimentation, and hesitation into action.

The Freelancer Who Became an Entrepreneur

Take Ankur Warikoo, for example. Early in his career, he could have stayed in secure corporate jobs. But he embraced risk, experimented with ideas, and built businesses and side hustles that eventually gave him both wealth and freedom.

Or think of Russell Brunson: he started with small online funnels while many laughed at the idea of internet marketing. Today, his systems generate millions, all because he acted despite the unknown.

The lesson? **Breaking limiting beliefs is the first step from being an earner to becoming a builder.**

Practical Steps to Shift Your Mindset

Identify Your Limiting Beliefs

- Write down 5 beliefs about money, success, or risk that hold you back.

Challenge Them

- For each belief, ask: *"Is this really true, or just what I've been told?"*

Replace With Empowering Beliefs

- Example:
- Old belief: "I can't start a business; I don't have enough money."
- New belief: "I can start small, learn fast, and scale gradually."

Take Small, Calculated Risks

- Start a micro side hustle, invest a small amount, or learn a skill you can monetize.

Exercise: From Earner to Builder

1. List **3 ways you currently earn money**.
2. Brainstorm **3 ways to build systems** that earn money without trading hours.
3. Choose **one idea** and take a small action this week—set up a mini test, make a small investment, or learn a critical skill.
4. Reflect on progress at the end of the week. Success isn't instant—it's consistent action that compounds.

Key Takeaway

Being an earner keeps you safe—but building wealth requires courage, calculated risks, and breaking the invisible chains of limiting beliefs. The shift from earner to builder is **less about money and more about mindset**.

Remember: **every millionaire you admire once took that first step despite fear**. Your journey begins the moment you decide to act.

Actionable Step for This Week:

- Identify one limiting belief about money, career, or risk.
- Write down **one small action** to challenge it this week.
- Take that action and note your learning—it's the start of your transformation from earner to builder.

6

The Power of Taking Calculated Risks

"R*isk is not the enemy of wealth. Fear of risk is."*

Most middle-class people avoid risk like it's a virus. Safe jobs, predictable routines, and steady salaries feel comforting—but they rarely lead to real financial freedom. If you want to escape the 9–5 trap and build wealth, **risk is inevitable**. The key is learning to take **calculated, smart risks**, not reckless gambles.

Risk vs. Reckless Gambling

Let's simplify it:

- **Reckless Gambling**: Jumping into something with no knowledge, preparation, or plan. Example: investing your life savings in a random cryptocurrency because "everyone's making money."
- **Calculated Risk**: Taking small, informed steps where the downside is manageable, and the potential upside is worth it. Example: investing ₹5,000 to start a small freelance service or online shop while keeping your job.

Here's a rule I follow: **never risk what you can't afford to lose**, but **always**

invest time, energy, and small resources to explore opportunities. That's how wealth grows without unnecessary stress.

The Magic of Small Risks

I remember my first calculated risk vividly. I was earning a steady salary and could have stayed comfortable forever. But I decided to try a small freelance project online. The project cost me almost nothing in money but a lot in learning and effort.

Result? I earned my **first ₹10,000 from a side hustle**, and more importantly, I discovered I **could make money outside my salary**. That tiny risk changed my mindset forever. I realized: *wealth isn't about luck—it's about action and calculated experimentation.*

Real-Life Story: From Zero to First Revenue

Take Priya, a friend of mine. She was a college graduate working a 9–5 in marketing. One day, she decided to sell handmade products online—a tiny side hustle she thought would "just cover expenses." She invested a small ₹2,000 in materials, spent evenings learning online marketing, and reached her first ₹10,000 revenue within a month.

Priya's risk was **small, smart, and manageable**. But the confidence and mindset shift she gained? Priceless. That first small success gave her courage to scale bigger, take more calculated risks, and explore additional income streams.

Why Calculated Risk is Essential for Wealth

Middle-class life teaches us: *avoid mistakes at all costs.* But avoiding all risks also **avoids opportunity**. Every millionaire you admire took small, smart risks before scaling. They experimented, learned, and grew.

A simple mindset to adopt:

"If I act smartly and take manageable steps, failure is a lesson, and success is inevitable."

Reflection Exercise: Identify One Small Risk

Look at your current situation. What is one "safe zone" or comfort area holding you back?

Ask: "What is a small step I can take this month to challenge it?"

Examples:

- Offer your skill online as a freelancer.
- Invest ₹1,000–₹5,000 in learning a new income-generating skill.
- Start a small online store or digital service trial.

Write it down, commit, and take action this week.

Step-by-Step Approach to Risk-Taking

1. **Identify Opportunity** – Where can you earn, learn, or grow?
2. **Assess Downside** – What's the worst-case scenario if it fails? Can you handle it?
3. **Start Small** – Risk small amounts of money, time, or energy.
4. **Learn Fast** – Treat failures as lessons. Iterate and improve.
5. **Scale Gradually** – Once confident, expand your risk in controlled ways.

I used this approach to gradually shift from my secure salary to multiple side hustles and eventually full-scale digital businesses. Each calculated risk compounded into bigger results over time.

Key Takeaway

Wealth isn't about avoiding risk—it's about **taking calculated risks that can grow your income and confidence**. The first step is often the hardest, but once you see results—even small ones—the mindset shift happens naturally.

Actionable Step for This Month:

- Pick **one small calculated risk** you can take this month.
- Take **concrete action**: start a side hustle, launch a small project, or invest in learning a marketable skill.
- Track progress, celebrate small wins, and reflect on lessons.

7

Time Freedom > Money Traps

"You can earn more money, but if your time is fully consumed, you'll never truly be free. Time is the ultimate currency."

Most middle-class people fall into the **money trap**: trading every hour for a fixed salary. The logic seems sound—more hours, more pay—but here's the catch: **your earning potential is capped**. No matter how hard you work, your time ends at 24 hours a day. If you want to break free and build real wealth, **time freedom is more valuable than money**.

Why Trading Hours for Money Caps Growth

Think about it:

- You work 8–10 hours a day for your employer.
- You earn ₹30,000–₹50,000 per month.
- Even if you double your hours or switch to a higher-paying job, your earning potential grows linearly.

Meanwhile, entrepreneurs and side-hustlers multiply their income using **systems, digital tools, and leverage**, where 1 hour of effort can create money long after that hour is gone.

I experienced this myself. Early in my career, I worked extra hours thinking it would accelerate my growth. But at the end of the month, my income didn't reflect the extra effort. It felt exhausting, limiting, and frustrating. That's when I realized: **time is the bottleneck**, not effort.

The Power of Side Hustles

A side hustle allows you to **invest small chunks of time**—even 1 hour a day—into creating **sustainable revenue streams**. The beauty? Over time, these hours compound into:

- Digital products that sell while you sleep
- Freelance services that generate passive leads
- Skills that scale beyond your local market

I started my first side hustle by dedicating **just 1 hour a day** after my full-time job. Within weeks, I had my first ₹5,000–₹10,000 revenue. By month three, I was earning more than my salary from these small efforts. That tiny investment of time multiplied in ways my salary never could.

Mini Checklist: 1 Hour/Day to Side Hustle Success

Goal: Dedicate at least 1 hour/day to building your first side hustle.

1. **Plan Your Hour** – Choose a consistent time daily (before work, after work, or lunch breaks).
2. **Pick a Side Hustle Idea** – Freelancing, digital services, content creation, small online business.
3. **Take Action** – Complete one small task: create a profile, send proposals, design a product.
4. **Track Progress** – Note revenue earned, skills gained, or leads generated.
5. **Reflect Weekly** – Ask: "What worked? What can I improve?"

Even a single hour consistently invested grows exponentially over time. It's not about working harder—it's about **working smarter with leverage**.

Real-Life Story: From Salary Trap to Time Freedom

I remember Priya, a 26-year-old working woman, stuck in a 9–5 marketing job. She loved her job but wanted financial freedom. She started a small Etsy shop, dedicating **1 hour daily** after office hours. Within two months, she had her first ₹12,000 revenue, and by the sixth month, it became a **steady ₹40,000/month extra income**, all while keeping her job.

The lesson? **Time invested wisely beats money earned mindlessly.**

Reflection Exercise

1. Identify 1 hour/day you can dedicate to a side hustle.
2. Write down a **small, achievable task** you can complete each day for this side hustle.
3. Commit to tracking your progress for 30 days.
4. At the end of the month, evaluate your revenue, skills, and confidence growth.

Key Takeaway

The middle-class mindset focuses on **earning more money by working more hours**, but true wealth comes from **creating systems and side hustles that free your time**. Time is the ultimate leverage, and even 1 hour/day can set you on the path to financial freedom.

Actionable Step for This Week:

- Block 1 hour/day in your schedule for your first side hustle.
- Identify **one small task** to complete each day.
- Start today, track results, and reflect weekly. Small steps compound into massive results.

8

Finding Your Side Hustle

"T*he first step to wealth isn't making millions—it's discovering the right small opportunity that aligns with your skills, passion, and market needs."*

By now, you understand the importance of **mindset, calculated risk, and investing your time wisely**. But the next question is: *What side hustle should I start?*

The truth is, most middle-class people never ask themselves this. They wait for "the perfect idea" or "the right time," which rarely comes. The key is **starting small with what you already know or enjoy**, then growing it systematically.

Examples of Side Hustles You Can Start Today

Here are practical ideas that people in your situation—housewives, working professionals, freelancers, or recent graduates—can start **without huge investments**:

Freelancing

- Writing, graphic design, video editing, social media management.
- Platforms: Fiverr, Upwork, Freelancer.

Content Creation

- Blogging, YouTube channels, newsletters, or podcasts.
- Focus on topics you are passionate about; monetize later via ads, affiliate marketing, or courses.

Small Digital Businesses

- Selling handmade products, printables, digital templates, or online courses.
- Low-cost platforms like Etsy, Gumroad, or Shopify can help you start quickly.

Coaching / Consulting

- Teaching a skill you already know, like language lessons, fitness training, or career mentoring.
- Start with friends, family, or local groups; expand online gradually.

Service-Based Side Hustles

- Pet-sitting, tutoring, virtual assistance, local delivery services, or event management.

Discovering Your Skill or Interest

Before jumping in, ask yourself a few guiding questions to identify the **right side hustle for you**:

What skills do I already have?

- Consider both professional and personal skills. Example: If you're good at Excel, could you offer freelancing data services?

What do I enjoy doing?

- Passion helps you sustain effort over time. Small interest today can turn into revenue tomorrow.

What problems can I solve for others?

- Every business solves a problem. Identify pain points in your circle or community.

What resources or tools do I already have?

- Laptop, camera, craft materials, internet, or even your social network.

What can I realistically start with minimal risk?

- Start small; don't wait for perfection. The first step is **action**, not perfection.

How I Found My First Side Hustle

I remember sitting at my desk, tired of the 9–5 routine but unsure what to do. I listed my skills and passions and realized I could teach small online marketing strategies to beginners. I started with **one client, offering advice for ₹500 per session**.

It was small, but it built my confidence and gave me real-world experience. Within three months, I had **multiple clients and a recurring side income**, and my first small venture eventually grew into a larger online business. The point? **Start with what you know, and build gradually.**

Exercise: Discover Your Side Hustle

1. Write down **all your skills**, no matter how small.
2. Circle the top **3 skills you enjoy most**.
3. Ask: *"Who would pay me for this skill or service?"*
4. Pick **one skill to start experimenting with this month**.
5. Take **one small action**: reach out to a potential client, create a product, or offer a free trial.

Key Takeaway

The right side hustle is **not about chasing the biggest trend or earning fast**—it's about **starting with what you know, what you enjoy, and what solves real problems**. Every big entrepreneur began with a small, imperfect first step.

Start small. Act fast. Learn as you go. Your first small hustle is the foundation of your journey toward time freedom and financial independence.

Actionable Step for This Week:

- Answer the 3–5 guiding questions to identify your potential side hustle.
- Take **one concrete action** to start testing it within your available 1-hour daily time block.
- Reflect at the end of the week: note what worked, what didn't, and your excitement level.

9

Money Mindset for Beginners

"It's not how much you earn—it's how much you keep, grow, and reinvest."

Most middle-class people think financial success comes from **earning more money**. The truth? If you earn ₹50,000/month but spend ₹50,000/month, wealth will **never accumulate**. The foundation of any side hustle or business journey is a **strong money mindset**, and that starts with **saving, budgeting, and reinvesting your earnings wisely**.

Step 1: Change Your Relationship With Money

Money isn't just cash—it's **a tool to create freedom and opportunities**. Many people treat money as a source of stress, fear, or guilt. The shift begins with seeing money as a **lever**, not a limit.

Here's what I learned early in my journey:

- Every rupee saved and invested wisely compounds into larger opportunities.
- Small wins today build the confidence to take bigger financial actions tomorrow.
- Mindset beats numbers—if your thinking is wrong, your bank balance will reflect it.

Step 2: Saving and Budgeting Made Simple

Even beginners can start with **3 simple rules**:

Track Your Income and Expenses

- List your salary, side hustle earnings, and monthly expenses.
- Awareness creates control.

Follow the 50-30-20 Rule (Simple Version)

- 50%: Essentials (food, rent, bills)
- 30%: Lifestyle (fun, dining, entertainment)
- 20%: Savings & Investments

Automate Savings

- Even ₹500–₹1,000 per week saved automatically can snowball over months.

Personal example: When I started my first side hustle, I earned my first ₹10,000. Instead of spending it all, I saved ₹5,000 and invested ₹5,000 into growing my side hustle further. Within two months, my income **doubled**, just because I reinvested and didn't splurge.

Step 3: Reinvesting Small Wins

Reinvestment is the key to compounding growth:

- **Example 1:** Freelancing earnings → Upgrade tools, courses, or ads to reach more clients.
- **Example 2:** Small online business → Improve product quality or marketing.

- **Example 3:** Content creation → Invest in software or ads to grow audience faster.

Even small reinvestments lead to exponential results over time. This is how small wins snowball into serious income streams.

The Power of Small Wins

Ravi, a friend and a college graduate, started a simple freelance graphic design side hustle. He earned his first ₹2,000 in a week. Most people would have spent it on gadgets or food, but he saved ₹1,000 and used the rest to run small Facebook ads for his services. Within two months, his earnings grew to ₹15,000/month.

The lesson? **Every small win reinvested builds momentum.**

Exercise: Build Your Beginner Money Mindset

1. **Track your earnings** for the next 2 weeks (salary + side hustle).
2. **List all expenses** during that period.
3. **Decide 20% to save or reinvest**, even if it's a small amount.
4. **Choose one way to reinvest**: learning, marketing, tools, or small business expense.
5. **Reflect weekly**: Did reinvesting create opportunities or increase earnings?

Key Takeaway

Your **mindset about money** determines whether small wins grow or vanish. The first step to financial freedom is not earning more—it's **saving, budgeting, and reinvesting consistently**. Even ₹500–₹1,000 invested wisely every week can become a small empire in a year.

Actionable Step for This Week:

- Track all your income and expenses.
- Allocate at least 20% for savings or reinvestment.
- Take one small action to grow your earnings using that reinvestment.

10

Small Wins Build Confidence

"*Confidence isn't born—it's earned, one small win at a time."*

Middle-class life teaches patience and caution. But when it comes to **building wealth or side hustles**, patience without action can become procrastination. The key to breaking out of the 9–5 trap is **creating small, measurable wins that build confidence and momentum**. Each win, no matter how minor it seems, reinforces your belief: *I can do this.*

Why Small Wins Matter

Imagine your side hustle journey as climbing a mountain. If you aim to reach the summit in one leap, you'll likely fail. But if you focus on **one step at a time**, the climb becomes manageable.

Small wins:

- Reduce fear of failure. Each success proves risk is manageable.
- Build skill and knowledge. Repeated action develops expertise.
- Strengthen mindset. Confidence compounds like money.

Personal story: When I first started my side hustle, earning ₹500–₹1,000 a week felt tiny. But each time I earned something, **I gained clarity, motivation, and belief in my ability to create income outside my salary**. After three months, I reached my first ₹10,000 milestone. That was a game-changer. It wasn't the money—it was **the confidence it built**.

Case Study: First ₹10k/month → Scaling Mindset

Let's take Ravi, a college graduate who wanted financial freedom but was trapped in a small 9–5 job. He started a freelance graphic design service with minimal investment and set a **target of ₹2,000/week**.

- **Week 1:** Earned ₹1,800 → small win, minor adjustment in pricing.
- **Week 2:** Earned ₹2,300 → reinforced confidence and process.
- **Week 4:** Earned ₹5,000 → realized side hustle can actually generate meaningful income.

By **month 2**, Ravi hit **₹10,000 in monthly revenue**. The most important result wasn't just the money—it was **his mindset shift**: he saw that consistent effort + reinvestment = scalable results.

The Psychology Behind Small Wins

- **Momentum Principle:** Success breeds motivation. Each small win makes the next action easier.
- **Fear Reduction:** Early wins prove that risk is manageable.
- **Skill Compounding:** Small actions repeated daily develop expertise faster than sporadic big leaps.

Even small victories, like earning your first ₹1,000 online, build confidence that allows you to **scale bigger and take smarter risks**.

How to Identify Small Wins

1. **Revenue-Based Wins** – Achieve your first ₹1,000, ₹5,000, or ₹10,000 milestone.
2. **Skill-Based Wins** – Learn a new marketing skill, design template, or social media tactic.
3. **Process Wins** – Complete 5 client proposals, launch your first product, or schedule your daily hour consistently.

Rule of Thumb: Wins must be **achievable, measurable, and repeatable**.

Exercise: List 3 Small Wins to Achieve in 30 Days

Write down 3 small, specific goals for your side hustle this month. Examples:

- Earn ₹2,000 from your first freelance project.
- Create and launch your first digital product.
- Reach 50 followers/subscribers on a content platform.

Break each goal into daily micro-actions. Example:

- Reach out to 2 potential clients per day.
- Design 1 product template every 2 days.
- Post 3 helpful content pieces per week.

Track progress daily. Celebrate every small achievement—it trains your brain to see success as achievable.

Scaling Mindset Through Wins

Once you achieve small wins:

- **Reinvest Time and Money** – Use profits or hours to grow your side hustle.
- **Raise Ambitions Gradually** – Double targets after consistent wins.
- **Reflect and Adjust** – Learn from what worked and iterate for better results.

I remember hitting ₹10,000 in my first digital venture. That milestone was modest financially, but the **confidence it gave me was priceless**. I started thinking bigger, planning strategically, and eventually building multiple revenue streams.

Key Takeaway

Small wins are **not just milestones—they're mindset builders**. Each measurable success proves:

- I can earn outside a 9–5.
- My efforts create tangible results.
- Scaling is possible if I repeat and improve.

Remember: confidence compounds just like money. **Every ₹100 earned, every skill learned, every task completed is a brick in the foundation of your future freedom.**

Actionable Step for This Week:

- List 3 measurable wins you want to achieve in the next 30 days.
- Break each into micro-actions you can execute in **your 1-hour daily side hustle block**.
- Take action and track progress daily. Celebrate each win.

11

Scaling Your Hustle

"Your side hustle isn't just a hobby—it's the first step toward financial independence and creating multiple streams of income."

Many middle-class people stop at earning a little extra from a side hustle. They're happy with a few thousand extra, thinking: *"This is enough."* But here's the truth: **side hustles are stepping stones, not the destination**. If you want financial freedom, you need to **scale them systematically**.

Step 1: From Side Hustle to Main Income

The first stage of scaling is **building consistency and reliability**:

- Earn your first ₹10k/month regularly.
- Treat your side hustle like a small business, not a part-time hobby.
- Reinforce habits: daily actions, client follow-ups, and delivering quality results.

My first freelance client paid me ₹500. That seemed small. But I treated that project like it mattered—communicated clearly, delivered fast, and asked for feedback. By repeating this process with multiple clients, my side hustle **grew to replace my full-time salary within 6 months**.

Key principle: **consistency** > **size**. Small, reliable income streams compound over time.

Step 2: Build Systems to Multiply Income

Once you've stabilized income, focus on **systems and leverage**:

- **Automation:** Use simple tools to schedule social media posts, automate emails, or manage client communication.
- **Templates and Packages:** Standardize services or products so you can handle more clients or sales without burning out.
- **Delegation:** Hire freelancers, virtual assistants, or collaborators for repetitive tasks.

Example: I created a **template-based digital marketing service**. One hour of setup allowed me to serve 5–10 clients per week with minimal extra effort. The leverage turned small earnings into scalable income.

Step 3: Diversify Into Passive Income Streams

True freedom comes when your hustle earns even while you sleep:

1. **Digital Products:** Templates, courses, or ebooks.
2. **Affiliate Marketing:** Recommend tools or services you use.
3. **Subscription Models:** Monthly memberships or services.

Case study: Ankur Warikoo started freelancing but diversified into **digital products and online courses**. Today, he earns passive revenue streams alongside his active consulting.

Step 4: Mindset Shift for Scaling

Scaling isn't just about money—it's **a mindset shift**:

- Move from thinking **"I need to earn more now"** to **"How can I create systems to earn more without adding hours?"**
- Accept that initial efforts may be uncomfortable. Growth comes outside the comfort zone.
- Focus on **impact and value**, not just transactions.

I remember scaling my first side hustle by creating **a simple client onboarding system**. Initially, it felt tedious, but it freed hours weekly, allowed more clients, and increased revenue exponentially. The lesson: **work smarter, not harder.**

Exercise: Map Your Side Hustle Growth

1. Write down your current side hustle activities.
2. Identify **1–2 tasks that can be automated**.
3. Identify **1–2 tasks that can be delegated**.
4. Brainstorm **1 passive income opportunity** related to your hustle.
5. Create a simple plan to implement one change this week.

Small Wins → Big Results

Scaling is a **step-by-step journey**:

- Step 1: Earn consistently from your side hustle.
- Step 2: Automate, systemize, and delegate.
- Step 3: Introduce passive income streams.
- Step 4: Continuously reinvest and improve.

Every top entrepreneur started small. Freelancers became entrepreneurs, products became businesses, and small wins turned into consistent, scalable revenue streams.

Key Takeaway

Your side hustle is **the foundation of your financial freedom**. By treating it as a business, building systems, and diversifying income streams, **small efforts today can transform into long-term wealth and independence**.

Actionable Step for This Week:

- List all your hustle tasks. Identify **one you can automate** and **one you can delegate**.
- Brainstorm **one passive income idea** to start testing within 30 days.
- Commit to taking action and track progress.

12

The Millionaire Mindset for Long-Term Growth

"E*arning money is temporary. Thinking like a millionaire makes it permanent.*"

By now, you've started a side hustle, celebrated your first small wins, and even scaled some of your efforts. But the real transformation comes when you **shift your mindset from short-term earnings to long-term wealth creation**.

Most middle-class people work hard for **monthly paychecks**, then spend almost all of it. The mindset of a millionaire is **different**: it focuses on **earning, saving, reinvesting, and creating multiple revenue streams** that grow independently of hours worked.

Step 1: Think Beyond the Paycheck

The first trap is seeing money as a **linear exchange**: hours = salary.
Millionaires think differently:

- Money is a **tool to create leverage**.

- Time is finite, so income must eventually **work for you**, not the other way around.
- Risks are **calculated, not reckless**, and every decision is measured for long-term growth.

Personal example: When I was earning my first ₹10k/month from freelancing, I didn't just spend it. I **reinvested 50% into learning new skills, marketing, and tools**, while saving the rest. That decision compounded my income faster than my 9–5 salary ever could.

Step 2: Reinvest, Don't Spend

Reinvestment is the **heart of millionaire thinking**. Every rupee you invest wisely is a seed for bigger growth:

- **Skill Development:** Learn marketing, sales, or tech tools that increase earning potential.
- **Business Expansion:** Reinvest earnings into products, services, or marketing campaigns.
- **Passive Income:** Develop digital products, online courses, or affiliate income.

Case study: Rohan, a middle-class freelancer, earned his first ₹20k online. Instead of buying a new phone or taking a vacation, he invested ₹10k in running ads for his services and used the rest to buy online courses. Within three months, his income **tripled**, and he had a plan for recurring revenue.

Lesson: Spending small wins can feel satisfying, but reinvesting them **accelerates growth and builds financial confidence**.

Step 3: Multiple Revenue Streams Are Essential

One income source is risky. Millionaires build **ecosystems of money**, including:

1. **Active Income:** Freelancing, services, or consulting.
2. **Semi-Passive Income:** Selling products, digital templates, or subscriptions.
3. **Passive Income:** Affiliate marketing, royalties, or investments in stocks/crypto.

Personal touch: I started with one small side hustle. Then I launched a digital product, created a membership subscription, and later invested in low-risk online businesses. Each stream reinforced the others, giving me **financial stability and exponential growth**.

Step 4: Long-Term Thinking & Patience

Middle-class culture teaches impatience: "I need results now." Millionaires think **long-term**:

- Wealth compounds slowly at first.
- Early sacrifices (time, luxury, comfort) pay off in later freedom.
- Avoid "get-rich-quick" traps; focus on **consistent, measurable growth**.

Case study: Priya, a college graduate, earned ₹5,000/month from freelancing. She resisted the temptation to splurge and saved ₹3,000/month for six months. By the end of the year, she had **enough to start a small digital product business**, which later became her primary income.

Step 5: Mindset Exercises for Long-Term Growth

Financial Reflection:

- Track every rupee earned, saved, and reinvested this month.
- Ask: "How did my money work for me?"

Diversification Exercise:

- List your current income streams.
- Identify 1 new stream you can start this quarter.

Compound Thinking:

- Write down 3 ways small wins can grow over 6–12 months.
- Visualize the impact if repeated consistently.

Key Takeaways

- Millionaire mindset = **long-term thinking, reinvestment, and multiple income streams**.
- Small wins + reinvestment = **momentum and confidence**.
- Patience and persistence beat shortcuts every time.

Personal reminder: Every millionaire I know started small—sometimes with **₹500 or less in hand**—but their thinking, patience, and willingness to reinvest made them unstoppable. You can do the same.

Actionable Steps for This Week:

1. Review your current income and side hustle results.
2. Decide **one area to reinvest** for growth (skills, marketing, or tools).
3. Brainstorm **one additional income stream** you can start within the

next 30 days.

4. Write down your 6-month goal and visualize your financial freedom.

13

Mastering Time & Productivity for Side Hustle Growth

"Time is your most valuable currency—spend it wisely, and it will multiply your income and freedom."

One of the biggest obstacles for middle-class earners and side hustlers is **time**. Most are juggling:

- A full-time job or college
- Family responsibilities
- Household chores
- Social commitments

How can anyone build a side hustle or multiple income streams with such limited hours? The answer: **mastering time and productivity**, not working harder.

Step 1: The 1-Hour Daily Rule

You don't need 8-hour workdays to grow a side hustle. Even **1 focused hour daily** can create momentum.

Personal example: During my early freelancing days, I had a full-time job and family responsibilities. I dedicated **just one hour every evening** to my side hustle. Within six months, that hour generated **₹10,000–₹15,000 monthly**, proving that **consistent micro-efforts beat sporadic marathon sessions**.

Tip: Treat this hour like a non-negotiable meeting with your future self.

Step 2: Prioritize High-Impact Tasks

Most people waste energy on low-value activities: checking emails, scrolling social media, or doing repetitive tasks. Use the **80/20 rule (Pareto Principle)**:

- 20% of tasks create 80% of results.
- Identify the **top 3 tasks** daily that directly grow income or skill.
- Delegate, automate, or postpone the rest.

I used to spend hours sending cold emails manually. Later, I automated them and focused on **client calls and delivering work**—my income **doubled without extra hours**.

Step 3: Batch Work for Efficiency

Batching similar tasks saves mental energy and time:

- Example: Create all social media posts for the week in one session.
- Example: Process client communications in two focused blocks per

day.

- Example: Record multiple videos at once instead of daily filming.

When you batch work, you reduce **decision fatigue** and **increase focus** on tasks that matter most.

Step 4: Use Time Blocks and Routines

Time-blocking helps middle-class hustlers balance work, family, and side projects:

1. Morning: 30–60 min for learning or skill-building.
2. Evening: 1 hour for client work, content creation, or side hustle tasks.
3. Weekends: 2–3 hours for scaling, planning, or creating passive income streams.

Personal touch: I blocked 7–**8 pm daily** for my digital business tasks. Initially, it felt tough, but my **consistent habit led to first ₹50k/month revenue**, even while working full-time.

Step 5: Avoid Burnout – Work Smarter, Not Longer

Scaling too quickly leads to burnout. Millionaire-minded hustlers:

- Focus on **sustainable routines**.
- Take breaks and recharge; avoid sacrificing health or relationships.
- Automate and delegate early to free time for **growth-focused work**.

Case study: Sneha, a middle-class working mother, struggled with side hustles alongside her job and household chores. She started time-blocking 1 hour daily and batching tasks. Within three months, her earnings doubled without extra stress, proving **small, smart time investments work wonders**.

Exercise: Your Weekly Productivity Plan

1. List all activities related to your side hustle this week.
2. Identify the **top 3 high-impact tasks** that will grow your income or skill.
3. Assign **time blocks** for each task. Example: 7–8 pm daily or 2–4 pm weekend.
4. Identify **1 task to automate or delegate**.
5. Track daily productivity and celebrate completion of your high-impact tasks.

Step 6: Mindset Shift – Value Your Time Like Money

Time = Money = Freedom. The more you value your **hourly effort**, the more likely you are to:

- Prioritize income-generating tasks.
- Invest in tools, learning, or help that saves time.
- Scale faster without burning out.

When I realized my 1-hour daily efforts were **worth ₹500–₹1,000/hour in potential growth**, I stopped procrastinating. That mindset allowed me to **multiply my side hustle income without working full-time hours**.

Key Takeaways

- **Consistency beats intensity**: 1 focused hour/day is better than sporadic long sessions.
- **Prioritize high-impact tasks** using the 80/20 rule.
- **Batch, block, and automate** to save energy and time.
- **Protect yourself from burnout**—growth is sustainable, not exhausting.

Actionable Step for This Week:

1. Choose **1-hour daily block** exclusively for your side hustle.
2. List **top 3 tasks** that will create the most impact this week.
3. Identify **1 task to automate or delegate**.
4. Track your productivity daily and reflect on progress every Sunday.

14

Think Big, Start Small

"Dreams without a plan remain wishes. Big visions need small, actionable steps to come alive."

Most middle-class people **dream of wealth and freedom**, but dreams alone won't get you there. They often think:

- "I'll earn a crore someday."
- "I'll start a business when I have more time or money."

The reality is that **massive success begins with small, deliberate actions**. Every millionaire you admire started with a **small step**, then scaled it consistently.

Step 1: Adopt a 10x Growth Mindset

A 10x mindset means **thinking beyond your current limitations**:

- Don't settle for incremental growth. Ask: "How can I **10x my results** with the same effort?"
- Shift from scarcity thinking → abundance thinking.
- Focus on **opportunities instead of obstacles**.

When I first started my side hustle, my initial goal was ₹10k/month. But then I asked myself: *"How can I realistically earn ₹1 lakh/month with the same foundation?"* This question forced me to **think bigger** while starting small, changing the trajectory of my business.

Step 2: Break Big Goals Into Small Actions

Big visions can feel **overwhelming**. The trick is to **divide them into manageable milestones**:

1. **6-month goal:** Small, achievable target to create momentum.
2. **1-year goal:** Intermediate milestone showing real progress.
3. **5-year goal:** Big-picture vision of wealth, freedom, and multiple income streams.

Example:

Time frame. Goal Example

6 months Earn ₹50k/month from side hustle consistently

1 year Launch digital product and reach ₹1 lakh/month

5 years. Multiple side hustles generating ₹10 lakh/month

Breaking goals down prevents **analysis paralysis** and makes success feel tangible.

Step 3: Start Small but Take Action Daily

You don't need a huge budget, office, or team to start:

- Start with **1 hour per day** on your side hustle.
- Focus on **high-impact tasks**.
- Track progress and adjust weekly.

Personal example: My first venture was **freelance consulting with ₹500**

initial investment—literally a domain name and a simple website. Starting small allowed me to **learn, experiment, and iterate** without risking financial disaster.

Step 4: Build a Feedback Loop

Success comes from **measuring, learning, and scaling**:

1. Track results weekly.
2. Reflect on what worked and what didn't.
3. Make small adjustments to improve efficiency or revenue.

A colleague started selling digital templates online. His first month earned only ₹2k. He analyzed customer feedback, tweaked his pricing and presentation, and within three months, revenue jumped to ₹15k/month. The **small improvements compounded into big growth**.

Step 5: Mindset Shifts to Think Big

- Stop saying: "I'm too small to make a difference."
- Shift thinking from **immediate comfort → long-term freedom**.
- Value learning, experimentation, and taking **calculated risks**.
- Celebrate **small wins**; they create confidence for bigger risks.

I always keep a journal with **small wins and lessons learned**. This practice keeps me motivated and prevents me from underestimating the impact of incremental growth.

Exercise: Your 6-Month, 1-Year, 5-Year Goals

6-Month Goal:

- Write down **one achievable target** for your side hustle or income.
- Example: "Earn ₹50k/month consistently."

1-Year Goal:

- Identify a **bigger milestone** that pushes your growth.
- Example: "Launch my first digital product."

5-Year Goal:

- Dream big, imagining **financial freedom and multiple income streams**.
- Example: "Have three side hustles generating ₹10 lakh/month and invest in assets for long-term wealth."

Daily Action Plan:

- List **1–2 tasks per day** that move you toward your 6-month goal.
- Track completion and celebrate progress weekly.

Key Takeaways

- **Dream big, start small:** Every massive success is a result of tiny, consistent actions.
- **Set measurable goals:** 6-month, 1-year, 5-year milestones guide your path.
- **Daily action compounds:** Even 1 hour/day can grow into ₹1 lakh/month if done consistently.
- **Learn and adjust:** Feedback loops turn small experiments into scalable income streams.

The biggest shift for me was realizing that **I didn't need a perfect plan or unlimited resources**—I just needed **clarity, focus, and consistent small steps**. Once I started, momentum and confidence followed naturally.

Actionable Step for This Week:

1. Write down your **6-month, 1-year, and 5-year financial goals**.
2. Identify **3 daily actions** that contribute directly to your 6-month goal.

Track progress and reflect every Sunday: What worked? What can be improved

15

Habits That Multiply Wealth

"S*uccess isn't magic—it's the result of daily habits repeated consistently over time."*

We all admire millionaires for their wealth, freedom, and influence. But wealth isn't a one-time event—it's **the natural outcome of small, consistent habits**. What you do daily determines whether you stay stuck in the middle-class trap or step into financial independence.

Step 1: Learning Every Day

Millionaires never stop learning. Knowledge compounds like money:

- Read books, articles, or blogs related to business, investing, or personal development.
- Watch tutorials or online courses to improve your skills.
- Talk to mentors or peers who are ahead of you.

I make it a habit to **read at least 30 minutes daily** on entrepreneurship, marketing, and wealth-building. Some of the strategies I share in this book came directly from ideas learned in those daily reading sessions.

Tip: Even 15–20 minutes a day adds up to 100+ hours in a year—a massive advantage over someone who learns only occasionally.

Step 2: Networking With Purpose

Your network can either **limit or multiply your wealth**.

- Surround yourself with people who **challenge and inspire you**.
- Attend meetups, webinars, or online communities in your niche.
- Offer help first—give value, then build relationships.

Case study: A friend of mine started attending **freelancing forums** and LinkedIn groups. Within six months, he got **three high-ticket clients** and a mentorship opportunity—all because of intentional networking.

Lesson: Wealth grows faster when you **connect with the right people and share value consistently**.

Step 3: Reinvesting and Building Assets

Habits of millionaires include consistently **reinvesting earnings**:

- Skills: Courses, coaching, certifications
- Tools: Software, automation, or marketing tools
- Business: Ads, product development, scaling efforts

Early in my journey, I earned my first ₹20k from freelancing. I **reinvested ₹10k into running ads and upgrading my skillset**, instead of spending on comfort. That reinvestment grew into **₹1 lakh/month within six months**.

Habit principle: Make **reinvestment automatic**, like paying a bill every month—your future self will thank you.

Step 4: Daily Micro-Habits That Multiply Wealth

1. **Morning reflection (5 minutes):** Set daily goals and affirm growth mindset.
2. **Learning block (30 minutes):** Read, watch, or listen to something related to your skill or business.
3. **Networking (10–15 minutes):** Reach out, comment, or engage meaningfully.
4. **Reinvestment tracking (5 minutes):** Note what you spent and reinvested today.
5. **Evening review (5 minutes):** Reflect on wins, lessons, and adjustments.

Consistency in these small habits **creates compounding results over months and years**.

Step 5: Mindset Shift – Habits Over Motivation

Motivation is temporary; habits are permanent.

- Don't rely on feeling motivated daily.
- Focus on **systematic routines** that move you forward, even on lazy or busy days.
- Track habits, celebrate wins, and refine for better outcomes.

I used to wait for inspiration to work on side projects. Once I switched to **fixed routines and micro-habits**, progress became unstoppable, even on stressful days.

Exercise: Create 3 New Wealth-Building Habits

Identify three habits you want to adopt that directly impact your wealth:

- Example: Reading 20 minutes/day, connecting with 2 potential clients weekly, reinvesting 20% of earnings.

Schedule daily time blocks for these habits.

Track consistency daily for 30 days and reflect on improvements.

Adjust or add new habits after 30 days for continuous growth.

Key Takeaways

- Wealth multiplies when you **learn, network, and reinvest daily**.
- Small, consistent habits compound over time—much faster than sporadic efforts.
- Systematic routines beat short-term motivation.
- Start small, track progress, and gradually **increase the impact** of each habit.

Actionable Step for This Week:

1. Pick **3 new wealth-building habits**.
2. Schedule time blocks for each habit.
3. Track daily for 7 days and review progress at the end of the week.
4. Celebrate completion of each habit to reinforce consistency.

16

Mindset for Scaling Multiple Income Streams

"*Don't put all your eggs in one basket—your mindset is the most valuable asset you can scale.*"

Many middle-class earners and side hustlers focus on **one income source**—a job or a single gig. This is comfortable, but it's also risky and limiting. True wealth comes from **diversifying your income streams** and building a mindset that can handle multiple ventures.

Step 1: Understand the Power of Multiple Income Streams

Relying solely on a job means:

- Income stops if you lose your job.
- Growth is capped by your salary.
- Financial freedom is delayed.

Contrast this with someone earning from multiple sources:

- **Freelancing income** for immediate cash flow

- **Digital products or content** generating passive income
- **Investments** compounding wealth over time

In my early days, I had freelancing gigs as my main income. When I started creating digital courses and offering consulting services, my revenue **tripled within a year**, even though I didn't work more hours.

Lesson: **Scaling income streams is more about strategy than harder work.**

Step 2: Mindset Shifts Needed for Scaling

Think abundance, not scarcity:

- Don't fear spreading efforts across multiple ventures.
- Resources, clients, and opportunities are abundant when approached strategically.

Embrace calculated risk:

- Small experiments in new income streams reduce fear and build confidence.
- Example: Investing ₹1,000 in a mini digital product launch rather than waiting for a perfect plan.

Learn to detach from single-source dependency:

- Your first stream is important but not sacred.
- Always test new ideas while maintaining stability in the main source.

I initially feared branching into affiliate marketing while freelancing. Once I **treated it as an experiment**, I realized it was adding **recurring revenue** without jeopardizing my existing income.

Step 3: Prioritize and Sequence Your Income Streams

Not all streams should start at once. Follow a sequence:

1. **Primary stream:** Stable and reliable.
2. **Secondary stream:** Medium-effort, medium-reward.
3. **Tertiary stream:** High-risk, high-reward opportunities.

Example roadmap:

Stream, Effort, Reward, Stage

Freelancing / Job Medium Medium Month 1–6

Digital products / Courses. High High Month 3–12

Investments / Assets Medium Compounding Month 6+

I began with a **freelance skill I already had**, then added a **digital course**, and finally **invested in tools and software** that generated passive returns. Each stream reinforced the others.

Step 4: Build Systems, Not Chaos

Multiple income streams can create **overwhelm** if not managed correctly:

- Track earnings and expenses for each stream.
- Automate repetitive tasks wherever possible.
- Delegate low-value activities to free up time for **growth-oriented work**.

Case study: Ankur, a middle-class entrepreneur I know, started with one client-based service. When he added a YouTube channel and e-book sales, he initially felt overwhelmed. By **tracking revenue, batching tasks, and using basic automation tools**, he scaled to **3–4 profitable income streams** without burning out.

Step 5: Mindset Habits for Multi-Stream Growth

1. **Daily reflection:** Review which streams are performing and where attention is needed.
2. **Learning allocation:** Spend 30–60 minutes daily learning strategies for scaling new income.
3. **Experimentation habit:** Test at least one new revenue idea every quarter.
4. **Risk tolerance journaling:** Record risks taken and lessons learned, building confidence over time.

I maintain a **growth journal** where I track experiments, wins, and failures for each income stream. This habit keeps me **strategic and disciplined** while scaling multiple ventures.

Exercise: Map Your Income Streams

1. List **all potential income sources** you can realistically pursue.
2. Rank them by **effort required vs. expected reward**.
3. Choose **1 primary, 1 secondary, and 1 tertiary stream** to focus on this quarter.
4. Set **milestones and timelines** for each stream: revenue targets, client goals, product launches, or investments.
5. Reflect weekly: Which streams are growing? Which need more focus?

Key Takeaways

- Wealth grows faster with **multiple income streams**; don't rely on one source.
- Sequence your efforts: start stable, add medium, then experiment with high-reward opportunities.
- Build **systems and habits** to manage complexity without burnout.
- Mindset is your strongest asset—think abundance, take calculated risks, and stay disciplined.

Actionable Step for This Week:

1. Write down **all potential income streams** you could start within your current capacity.
2. Pick **1 primary, 1 secondary, and 1 tertiary stream** to focus on this quarter.
3. Create a **mini weekly action plan** for each stream.

17

Avoiding Traps on the Road to Wealth

"The journey to wealth is not just about earning—it's about navigating the traps that can derail your progress."

Many middle-class earners and aspiring entrepreneurs **start with excitement and motivation**, only to get stuck in common traps that delay or even destroy their financial growth. Recognizing these pitfalls early is critical to **protect your journey**.

Trap 1: Procrastination

The biggest enemy of wealth is often **waiting for the "perfect time"**.

- Middle-class conditioning teaches: *"Wait until you have more money, time, or experience."*
- The truth: There is **no perfect moment**. Action creates momentum.

When I first wanted to start my side hustle, I delayed for months because I thought my skills weren't enough. One small decision—to offer my first service to a friend—changed everything. That tiny step built confidence and started the compounding effect of income and experience.

Exercise: List **one action you've been procrastinating** on for your side hustle. Take a **small step today**, no matter how imperfect.

Trap 2: Fear of Failure

Fear is natural but often paralyzing.

- Many middle-class people **avoid risk**, preferring stability.
- Fear of failure keeps you **stuck in low-paying jobs or side gigs**.

Story: A college friend of mine wanted to launch an online tutoring platform. Fear of losing ₹5,000 held him back. When he finally launched, he earned **₹50k in the first month**, learning more from mistakes than he ever imagined.

Mindset Shift: View failure as **feedback**, not judgment. Each mistake brings you closer to a scalable, profitable strategy.

Trap 3: Comparison and Envy

Comparison traps are subtle but dangerous:

- "Why is he earning more than me?"
- "I'll never be as successful as her."

These thoughts **consume energy**, distract from action, and create negative self-talk.

I used to compare my early freelancing earnings with top consultants. Instead of learning, I felt stuck. Once I **focused on my growth and small wins**, my income began compounding, and I realized comparison was stealing my progress.

Exercise: Write down **3 areas where you compare yourself** to others. For each, replace the thought with: *"I will focus on my progress and take one action today."*

Trap 4: Chasing Quick Wins

Many middle-class earners look for **fast money schemes**, hoping to bypass effort.

- Get-rich-quick schemes rarely lead to sustainable wealth.
- True wealth comes from **consistent learning, reinvestment, and compounding efforts**.

Story: A friend invested in a "get-rich-quick" online course, spending ₹20k upfront. After months, he had zero results. When he applied consistent freelancing and digital product strategies, he started earning **₹1 lakh/month**—a sustainable and scalable path.

Lesson: Wealth is built with **small, repeated, deliberate actions**, not shortcuts.

Trap 5: Overcommitting Without Focus

Taking on too many side hustles or projects without strategy can burn out your energy.

- Middle-class earners often feel they must **do everything at once**.
- Lack of focus dilutes results and slows progress.

Early in my journey, I tried freelancing, blogging, and affiliate marketing all at once. Nothing scaled. When I **focused on one primary income stream and a secondary experiment**, results multiplied.

Exercise: List all your current or planned income streams. **Choose one primary and one secondary focus** this quarter to maximize impact.

Key Mindset Shifts to Avoid Traps

1. **Start imperfectly:** Small action beats waiting for perfection.
2. **Fear is feedback:** Mistakes teach, they don't define you.
3. **Focus on growth, not comparison:** Track your wins, not others'.
4. **Consistency > shortcuts:** Repeated effort beats chasing quick wins.
5. **Prioritize focus:** One primary income stream scales faster than many scattered attempts.

Actionable Step for This Week:

1. Identify **one procrastination task**, one fear you're avoiding, and one area you compare yourself.
2. Take **one small, deliberate action** for each.
3. Track results and reflect: What did you learn? What can you improve?

"It's not just about working hard—it's about working smart and avoiding the mistakes that silently drain your growth."

As you take steps toward financial freedom, side hustles, and building multiple income streams, the middle-class mindset can trip you up. Many people **fall into invisible traps** that stop them from scaling, even when they work hard and are consistent. Recognizing these traps early is essential for **sustained wealth creation**.

Trap 1: Procrastination & Perfectionism

- Waiting for the "perfect time" or "perfect plan" is a trap.
- Middle-class earners often delay starting side hustles because of **fear, doubt, or analysis paralysis.**

I delayed launching my first digital product because I wanted the website, marketing, and content to be flawless. By the time I launched, I realized the **first version could have generated revenue months earlier**. Small, imperfect action beats perfect inaction every time.

Exercise: Identify **one task you've been postponing** and commit to completing it **within 48 hours**, no excuses.

Trap 2: Comparing Yourself to Others

- Social comparison steals focus, motivation, and confidence.
- Everyone's journey is different—what works for one may not work for you.

I used to compare my earnings to top freelancers in my niche. I felt inadequate until I **shifted focus to my growth and small wins**. Within months, my own revenue overtook what I had been comparing myself to.

Exercise: Write down **3 comparisons you make** and **replace them with 3 personal growth goals** instead.

Trap 3: Lifestyle Inflation

- Earning more but spending more keeps you **trapped in a cycle of work and bills**.
- Middle-class earners often feel the need to upgrade lifestyle as income rises.

Example: A friend earned his first ₹50k from freelancing and immediately bought a new phone, expensive clothes, and gadgets. His savings remained almost zero. Contrast that with another freelancer who **reinvested ₹30k into ads and courses**, scaling income to ₹2 lakh/month within six months.

Exercise: Track your **last 3 months of income vs. expenses**. Identify **1 expense you can cut** and **reinvest into growth**.

Trap 4: Fear of Risk & Change

- Comfort zones feel safe but **limit growth potential**.
- Side hustles require **calculated risk-taking**, not reckless gambling.

I remember hesitating to invest ₹5k into running my first ad campaign. Fear of loss held me back for a week. Once I finally invested, I earned ₹25k in revenue. Taking small, calculated risks is essential to move from **middle-class mindset to millionaire mindset**.

Exercise: Identify **one calculated risk** you can take this week—small, measurable, and reversible.

Trap 5: Lack of Systems and Processes

- Without simple systems, side hustles **consume all your time**.
- Middle-class earners often think "I can do it all myself," leading to burnout.

Tip: Automate repetitive tasks: invoicing, client follow-ups, social media posts, and content scheduling. Even **one hour of automation per week** frees time to scale your hustle.

Exercise: Make a **list of 3 repetitive tasks** in your side hustle/business and **find a way to automate or outsource** them this month.

Trap 6: Neglecting Learning & Networking

- Stagnation is a silent trap. Skills, knowledge, and connections are **your fastest growth multipliers**.
- Avoid the habit of doing everything in isolation—mentorship, communities, and peer learning **accelerate success**.

Story: I joined a small mastermind group early in my side hustle journey. Advice from peers helped me **avoid costly mistakes** and **scale faster**, something I would have struggled with alone.

Exercise: Reach out to **one mentor or peer** this week for advice or collaboration.

Trap 7: Giving Up Too Soon

- Wealth and financial independence are **marathon, not sprint**.
- Many middle-class earners quit after a few months of effort because **results aren't immediate**.

My first digital product earned just ₹2k in its first month. I could have given up, but consistent action and learning helped me reach ₹50k by the third month.

Exercise: Write down **3 reasons to persist** when progress feels slow. Refer to this list whenever you feel like quitting.

Mini Checklist – Avoiding Traps

1. Take action now, don't wait for perfect timing.
2. Stop comparing yourself; focus on personal growth.
3. Reinvest instead of inflating lifestyle.
4. Take small, calculated risks.

5. Build systems and automate repetitive tasks.
6. Invest in learning and networking.
7. Stay persistent; wealth compounds over time.

Key Takeaways

- Middle-class traps are subtle but powerful: procrastination, fear, comparison, and lifestyle inflation.
- Awareness is the first step—once recognized, these traps **can be avoided or turned into growth levers**.
- Action, persistence, reinvestment, and systems create the foundation for financial independence.
- Small, consistent steps compound into long-term wealth when aligned with the millionaire mindset.

Actionable Step for This Week:

1. Identify **2–3 traps you are currently falling into**.
2. Take **one immediate action** to avoid each trap this week.
3. Journal results and adjust for next week to ensure you stay on track.

18

The Power of Financial Independence

"True wealth isn't about how much you earn—it's about how much freedom you create for yourself."

Many middle-class earners spend decades trading time for money, believing that **a steady job, a promotion, or a raise** will eventually bring security. But true financial independence **doesn't come from working harder for someone else—it comes from creating systems, assets, and habits that work for you.**

Step 1: Understanding Financial Independence

Financial independence (FI) is not just having money—it's **having choices**.

- You can **decide how to spend your time**.
- You can **pursue opportunities** without financial fear.
- You can **invest in yourself, your family, or your business** without dependency.

When I first hit my first ₹1 lakh month from side hustles, I realized I didn't need to wait for a salary hike. That shift—knowing I could **earn, reinvest, and grow independently**—was empowering.

Key Principle: FI is about **building assets, not accumulating liabilities.**

Step 2: Calculate Your Freedom Number

Your "freedom number" is the **amount of passive income you need to cover your essential expenses.**

Exercise:

1. List **monthly essential expenses**: rent, bills, food, transportation, etc.
2. Multiply by 12 to get **annual requirement**.
3. Add a buffer (10–20%) for unexpected costs.

Your goal: Build income streams that **cover this number reliably**, even if your job income stops tomorrow.

Step 3: Convert Side Hustles into Systems

Side hustles are the first step, but **systems make them sustainable**:

- Automate repeatable tasks (email, marketing, client follow-ups).
- Use tools to track revenue, clients, and ROI.
- Standardize processes to scale without increasing hours.

My early freelancing work involved **manually sending proposals**. Once I built templates, automated outreach, and created SOPs, my revenue **scaled 5x without working extra hours**.

Step 4: Reinvest for Compounding Growth

Financial independence comes fastest when you **reinvest profits into new streams**.

- Skill development: Courses, mentorships, certifications
- Assets: Stocks, ETFs, real estate, or digital products
- Business growth: Ads, tools, outsourcing

I earned ₹10k from a small digital product. Instead of spending it on gadgets, I **invested ₹5k into running ads** and improving content quality. Within months, revenue jumped to ₹50k—a clear example of compounding effort.

Step 5: Build Multiple Revenue Streams for Stability

Don't rely on one income source:

1. **Primary:** Freelancing, job, or core business
2. **Secondary:** Digital products, services, or content monetization
3. **Tertiary:** Investments or passive income

Case study: A college friend started freelancing after graduation. Within a year, he added a **YouTube channel** and **affiliate marketing**. By the second year, passive streams **covered 60% of his expenses**, freeing him from fear of layoffs.

Step 6: Mindset Habits for Financial Independence

1. **Track every rupee:** Know where money comes and goes.
2. **Daily reflection:** Focus on growth, not comfort.
3. **Experiment regularly:** Test new side hustles or investment opportunities.
4. **Celebrate small wins:** ₹1k extra income today compounds to lakhs over time.
5. **Focus on assets, not liabilities:** Avoid lifestyle inflation traps.

I journal my income streams weekly and track reinvestments. This habit helps me **stay focused, disciplined, and confident**, even during slow months.

Step 7: Exercise – Create Your FI Plan

1. Calculate your **freedom number** (monthly expenses × 12 + buffer).
2. List **all current and potential income streams**.
3. Identify **1 primary, 1 secondary, and 1 tertiary stream** to scale this year.
4. Set milestones: monthly revenue targets, clients, or product launches.
5. Reflect monthly: What worked? What needs adjustment?

Key Takeaways

- FI is about **freedom, not just money**.
- Systems, habits, and multiple streams **compound your efforts**.
- Small, consistent reinvestments grow into life-changing results.
- Mindset is everything: focus on assets, take calculated risks, and experiment continuously.

Actionable Step for This Week:

1. Calculate your **freedom number**.
2. Identify **one stream to scale** and take one actionable step toward it today.
3. Journal your progress daily for one week to **build momentum**.

19

Think Big, Start Small

"Ambition without action is just a dream; small steps toward a big vision turn dreams into reality."

Many middle-class earners and aspiring entrepreneurs **have big dreams**—millionaire goals, financial freedom, or building a business empire—but struggle to **start because the vision feels too large**. The key is to **break your big goal into small, actionable steps** while keeping your eye on the ultimate prize.

Step 1: Embrace the 10x Mindset

Think beyond your current circumstances.

- Most people limit themselves to 2–3x growth because **comfort zones feel safe**.
- A **10x mindset** means aiming for goals that challenge and excite you.

I remember setting my first side hustle target: ₹50,000 per month. At the time, it felt impossible. But instead of shrinking the goal, I **broke it into weekly and**

daily actions. Small, consistent steps—sending proposals, creating content, connecting with clients—compounded into achieving the goal in just three months.

Mindset Shift: Don't shrink your dreams; **expand your actions**.

Step 2: Break Big Goals into Small Milestones

Big goals are overwhelming without a roadmap. Break them into manageable steps:

1. **6-month milestone:** Revenue target, number of clients, or product launches.
2. **1-year milestone:** Expand into multiple income streams or scale the main product.
3. **5-year milestone:** Achieve financial independence, automation, or team growth.

Exercise: Write down **one big financial goal**. Then **split it into three milestones**: 6 months, 1 year, and 5 years.

I used this technique when planning my digital business. Instead of targeting ₹1 crore immediately, I **set quarterly goals**, each one building confidence and revenue for the next.

Step 3: Start Small, Execute Consistently

- **Small actions compound over time**: 1 hour a day invested in your side hustle grows faster than random bursts of effort.
- Avoid paralysis by analysis—**perfect plans rarely exist**. Action trumps overthinking.

Example: A friend wanted to launch a YouTube channel but waited months to perfect scripts and editing. When he finally uploaded **just one video per week**, he started building an audience and income steadily.

Tip: Pick **one small action today** that moves you toward your big goal. Repeat daily.

Step 4: Test, Learn, and Adjust

Scaling requires experimentation:

- Track results for each action: What works? What doesn't?
- Adjust small actions based on feedback before scaling.
- Treat failures as experiments, not disasters.

When I launched my first digital course, I initially priced it too low. Early feedback from clients helped me **adjust content and pricing**, and by the second launch, revenue **quadrupled**. Small adjustments make a big difference.

Step 5: Stay Motivated with Vision and Reflection

- Keep your **big vision visible**—vision boards, journals, or reminders.
- Reflect weekly: celebrate small wins and assess what's moving you closer to your 10x goal.
- Accountability partners or mentors can accelerate your progress.

Exercise: Create a **weekly reflection sheet**:

1. What progress did I make this week?
2. What small wins can I celebrate?
3. What is my next small step toward my big goal?

I write a **weekly journal** every Sunday, summarizing progress, lessons, and the next week's actions. This keeps me aligned with long-term growth and prevents burnout.

Step 6: Actionable Mini-Checklist for Think Big, Start Small

1. Identify your **10x big goal**.
2. Break it into **6-month, 1-year, and 5-year milestones**.
3. Determine **small, daily or weekly actions** for each milestone.
4. Reflect weekly on progress, wins, and adjustments.
5. Repeat consistently, learning and compounding results.

Key Takeaways

- Big dreams are achievable when broken into small, actionable steps.
- Start small, execute consistently, test, learn, and adjust.
- Reflection and accountability accelerate progress.
- Mindset is the multiplier: **think 10x, act daily**.

Actionable Step for This Week:

1. Write down your **biggest financial goal for the next 5 years**.
2. Break it into **three milestones** (6 months, 1 year, 5 years).
3. List **3 small actions you can take this week** toward your 6-month milestone.

20

Habits That Multiply Wealth

"Wealth isn't built in a day—it's multiplied by the habits you practice every single day."

Big goals, small steps, and side hustles are important, but the **real multiplier for financial success** is your daily routine. Habits create momentum, automate success, and ensure that small actions compound into life-changing results.

Step 1: Morning Rituals that Set the Tone

How you start your day affects how productive and focused you are.

- Wake up with **purpose**: Decide the one priority for your day.
- Avoid distractions like social media for the first 30–60 minutes.
- Incorporate learning: Read, listen to podcasts, or watch short courses relevant to your skills or business.

I start my day at 5:30 AM, with 15 minutes of journaling, 15 minutes of planning, and 30 minutes of reading or listening to business podcasts. This simple habit ensures I **start every day aligned with my growth goals**, even before the world gets busy.

Exercise: Design your **morning routine for productivity and wealth-building**. Include at least 3 activities that directly improve your skills, mindset, or income streams.

Step 2: Focused Work Blocks

Time is the ultimate wealth multiplier.

- Use **time-blocking**: dedicate uninterrupted periods to your side hustle, learning, or business development.
- Avoid multitasking—it reduces efficiency and dilutes results.

Example: I used to check emails while creating content. Results? Slow progress and stress. Once I started **dedicated blocks for creation, outreach, and learning**, my output doubled in half the time.

Exercise: Schedule **2–3 focused work blocks per day**, even if only 30–60 minutes each, to work on your wealth-building actions.

Step 3: Continuous Learning & Skill Development

- Wealth grows faster for those who **upgrade their skills** regularly.
- Even 15–30 minutes per day adds up over a month: that's **7–15 hours of learning**—more than a weekend workshop.

When I first started my digital business, I spent just **20 minutes daily learning about funnels and automation**. Within 3 months, I implemented systems that generated my **first ₹50k in recurring income**.

Exercise: Pick **one skill** to improve this month that directly impacts your income or side hustle. Dedicate **15–30 minutes daily** to it.

Step 4: Reinvestment Habit

- Reinvest profits consistently into **your business, skills, or assets**.
- Even small reinvestments compound over time to significant wealth.

Example: From ₹10k earned in a small digital service, I reinvested ₹5k into improving content and running ads. Within a quarter, this generated **₹50k+ in revenue**, proving how reinvesting accelerates growth.

Exercise: Commit **10–20% of every side hustle or small income** to reinvestment. Track how it grows month over month.

Step 5: Networking & Relationships

- Wealthy habits include **building meaningful relationships**.
- Networking opens doors to collaborations, mentorships, clients, and growth opportunities.

One casual coffee chat led to a **freelance project worth ₹1.5 lakh**, which later became a long-term recurring client. Small investments in relationships yield exponential returns.

Exercise: Reach out to **one new person this week**—mentor, peer, or potential client. Build the habit of meaningful networking.

Step 6: Reflection & Journaling

- Weekly reflection ensures you **track progress, learn from mistakes, and reinforce positive habits**.
- Journaling even 10 minutes weekly helps internalize lessons, celebrate wins, and stay aligned with your 5-year vision.

Exercise: Every Sunday, write:

1. Wins this week (even small ones)
2. Lessons learned
3. Next week's key actions

Step 7: Mini Checklist – Habits That Multiply Wealth

1. Morning routine aligned with growth and learning.
2. Daily focused work blocks for your side hustle/business.
3. Skill-building for at least 15–30 minutes a day.
4. Reinvest a portion of profits consistently.
5. Network and nurture relationships weekly.
6. Weekly reflection and journaling.

Personal tip: Habits are the **compounding interest of personal growth**. Just like saving ₹100 daily compounds into lakhs over years, your habits—small, consistent, and aligned—multiply wealth over time.

Key Takeaways

- Daily habits are the **foundation for long-term financial independence**.
- Focus on routines that grow skills, income, and connections.
- Reinvest, reflect, and adjust consistently.
- Small, repeated actions compound into life-changing results.

Actionable Step for This Week:

1. Choose **3 habits to implement this week**: morning routine, focused work block, and reinvestment habit.
2. Track and journal daily progress.
3. Reflect weekly and adjust for maximum growth impact.

21

The Power of Financial Independence

"True freedom isn't earned by working harder; it's earned by making your money work for you."

Middle-class earners often trade **time for money**, believing that a stable job or paycheck is the only path to security. But **financial independence**—the ability to live without relying on a 9–5—is the ultimate game-changer. It's not about getting rich quickly; it's about **building systems, habits, and income streams** that allow you to choose how you spend your time.

Step 1: Understanding Financial Independence

Financial independence (FI) means:

- Your passive income covers your living expenses.
- You have the freedom to **choose how to spend your time**.
- You are no longer bound by fear of losing a job or paycheck.

I remember when I made my first ₹50k/month passively from digital products. It didn't make me a millionaire overnight, but it gave me **freedom to experiment, take risks, and grow**. That first taste of independence reshaped my mindset—now I measure success by **freedom, not just income**.

Exercise: Write down **what financial independence means to you**. How much monthly income would allow you to live freely?

Step 2: Multiple Streams of Income

Relying on one source of income is risky. The key to FI is **diversification**:

1. **Active income:** Freelancing, consulting, or side hustles.
2. **Passive income:** Digital products, affiliate revenue, or investments.
3. **Asset growth:** Real estate, stocks, or businesses that generate returns.

My journey to financial independence involved **starting small with freelancing**, then creating digital products, and eventually **building a small portfolio of recurring revenue streams**. Each layer multiplied my freedom.

Exercise: List your current income streams. Identify **one area to start creating a new passive stream**.

Step 3: The Habit of Reinvesting

Financial independence isn't about hoarding money—it's about **putting it to work**.

- Reinvest profits from your side hustle into **skills, tools, or products**.
- Small reinvestments compound over time into large growth.

I reinvested ₹10,000 from my first digital sale into a marketing course. That course helped me **double my revenue in two months**, which I then reinvested into ads—creating a compounding growth cycle.

Exercise: Commit **10–20% of every income earned** to reinvestment this month. Track growth over the next three months.

Step 4: Time Freedom & Lifestyle Design

Financial independence allows you to **choose your lifestyle**, not your job.

- Spend time on what you value: family, learning, travel, or passion projects.
- Avoid lifestyle inflation; increase freedom, not just consumption.

The first month I had my side hustles covering my essentials, I **traveled to a new city** while managing business remotely. The sense of freedom was addictive—it motivated me to **build more systems that generated income automatically**.

Exercise: Write down **three activities you'd do if money wasn't a constraint**. Plan small steps to integrate at least one of them this month.

Step 5: Mindset of Financial Independence

- Shift thinking from **salary-dependence to ownership and control**.
- Treat money as a tool, not a goal.
- Focus on **long-term freedom, not short-term comfort**.

Many middle-class earners avoid risk to stay "safe," but that comfort traps them. I took calculated risks with side hustles while keeping my job. The risk was small, but the mindset shift—seeing myself as an **owner, not just an employee**—was huge.

Exercise: Write down **one limiting belief about money or risk**. Then reframe it into a positive, growth-oriented belief.

Step 6: Mini Checklist – Path to Financial Independence

1. Define your **monthly income goal for independence**.
2. Identify and create **multiple income streams**.
3. Reinvest a portion of profits consistently.
4. Avoid lifestyle inflation; prioritize freedom over consumption.
5. Take calculated risks aligned with growth.
6. Reflect weekly and adjust actions for compounding results.

Key Takeaways

- Financial independence is **the ultimate freedom**, not just wealth.
- Small side hustles, reinvestment, and smart habits **compound into long-term freedom**.
- Time freedom, mindset, and multiple income streams are your core tools.
- Every small step toward independence **accelerates your journey from the middle-class trap to financial freedom**.

Actionable Step for This Week:

1. Calculate your **FI number** (monthly expenses fully covered by passive/side income).
2. List **1–2 small side hustles or investments** that can help reach this goal.
3. Take **one concrete action** toward creating or scaling that stream this week.

22

Your Personal 6-Month Action Plan

"A goal without a plan is just a wish. Now it's time to turn your millionaire mindset into measurable action."

By now, you've learned how to shift your mindset, start a side hustle, manage your money, and develop habits that multiply wealth. The next step is **creating a concrete plan to implement everything**. This 6-month action plan is designed for **middle-class earners, college grads, working professionals, and aspiring hustlers** who want to turn small steps into significant progress.

Month 1: Start Small, Take Action

Objective: Begin your journey, overcome fear, and take your first tangible steps.

1. **Mindset Reflection:** Write down your limiting beliefs and reframe them into growth-oriented statements.
2. **Identify a Side Hustle:** Choose one skill, interest, or small business idea to start this month.
3. **Set Up Basics:** Create a simple workspace, basic tools, or accounts needed for your side hustle.

4. **First Action Step:** Complete one task that generates initial traction—e.g., publish a gig, offer a service, or post your first social content.
5. **Reflection:** Journal your feelings, challenges, and wins at the end of the month.

Month 2: Build Consistency

Objective: Establish a routine and create measurable progress.

1. **Time Blocking:** Dedicate at least **1 hour daily** to your side hustle.
2. **Learning Habit:** Commit 15–30 minutes daily to improving a skill critical to your hustle.
3. **First Revenue:** Aim to earn your first small income (₹1k–₹5k) from your side hustle.
4. **Track Progress:** Record hours worked, tasks completed, and earnings to measure momentum.
5. **Reflection:** Note what worked, what didn't, and how you can improve.

Month 3: Small Wins, Big Confidence

Objective: Reinvest, scale, and gain confidence.

1. **Identify Small Wins:** List 3 actions you can complete this month to move closer to financial independence.
2. **Reinvestment:** Use part of your earnings to **upgrade tools, marketing, or learning resources**.
3. **Network & Learn:** Reach out to at least **one mentor or peer** for guidance.
4. **Systematize Tasks:** Identify repetitive tasks and explore automation or outsourcing.
5. **Reflection:** Journal wins, lessons learned, and momentum created.

Month 4: Scaling Your Side Hustle

Objective: Turn your side hustle into a growing income stream.

1. **Expand Offers:** Introduce additional services, products, or higher-value packages.
2. **Marketing & Visibility:** Share your services consistently on social media, freelance platforms, or via referrals.
3. **Revenue Target:** Aim to **double your monthly earnings** compared to Month 3.
4. **Track Metrics:** Start measuring ROI, hours vs income, and productivity efficiency.
5. **Reflection:** Note patterns of growth, bottlenecks, and new opportunities.

Month 5: Financial Management & Reinvestment

Objective: Build financial discipline and compound growth.

1. **Budget & Save:** Track all income and expenses; reinvest 10–20% into your hustle or learning.
2. **Passive Income Planning:** Identify small ways to generate recurring revenue.
3. **Habits Review:** Evaluate your routines—learning, focused work, and networking—and refine them.
4. **Mentorship Check:** Have a conversation with a mentor to validate progress and plan scaling strategies.
5. **Reflection:** Assess overall growth and adjust next month's plan to maximize results.

Month 6: Time Freedom & Long-Term Growth

Objective: Establish systems for sustainable income and financial independence.

1. **Automate & Delegate:** Implement simple automation or outsource tasks to free up your time.
2. **Scale Revenue:** Introduce upsells, packages, or higher-ticket offers to grow monthly income further.
3. **Set Next Milestones:** Define **6-month, 1-year, and 5-year financial goals**.
4. **Wealth Habits:** Revisit daily routines—learning, networking, and reinvesting—to ensure compounding growth.
5. **Reflection:** Write a summary of achievements, challenges, and actionable steps for continued growth.

Reflection Worksheet

Month, Key Actions, Wins, Challenges, Lessons Learned, Next Steps

1
2
3
4
5
6

Tip: Fill this table weekly to track progress and celebrate small wins. Your **small, consistent steps** compound into **significant financial freedom** over time.

Key Takeaways

- Action is more important than perfection—start small.
- Consistency compounds; dedicate focused time daily.
- Reinvest earnings and upgrade skills for exponential growth.
- Track, reflect, and adjust to stay aligned with long-term financial independence.
- Celebrate wins, however small, to stay motivated.

Summary / Key Takeaways

"Your journey from middle-class trap to financial freedom is a step-by-step process—small, consistent actions compound into long-term wealth."

1. **Mindset Shift Matters** – Beliefs about money, risk, and opportunity shape your results. Challenge limiting thoughts and adopt a growth mindset.
2. **Take Calculated Risks** – Small, smart risks accelerate your income and open opportunities others ignore.
3. **Side Hustles Are Your Launchpad** – Use them to test, learn, and grow income streams while maintaining safety nets.
4. **Reinvest, Don't Inflate** – Always put part of your income back into growth—skills, tools, or marketing.
5. **Consistency Beats Perfection** – Daily routines, time-blocking, and small wins compound into measurable progress.
6. **Avoid Traps** – Procrastination, fear, lifestyle inflation, and social comparison slow your growth. Awareness + action prevents setbacks.
7. **Financial Independence Is Freedom** – Aim for income streams that cover your essentials and let you choose how to spend your time.
8. **Think Big, Start Small** – Set ambitious yet achievable goals, scaling side hustles step by step.
9. **Habits Multiply Wealth** – Learning, networking, reinvesting, and maintaining productive routines accelerate results.

Reflection Exercises / Action Checklist

- List **3 limiting beliefs** about money and rewrite them into growth-focused statements.
- Identify **1 small risk** to take this week that could generate your first revenue.
- Commit **1 hour daily** to your side hustle for the next 30 days.
- List **3 passive income ideas** you can implement in the next 6 months.
- Track your **monthly income and expenses**, and plan 10–20% reinvestment into growth.
- Write down **3 small wins** to achieve this month and celebrate them.
- Set **6-month, 1-year, and 5-year financial goals**.

Tip: Use a journal or spreadsheet to track these exercises and revisit weekly to ensure progress.

FAQ for Beginners

Q1: I don't have any special skills. Can I still start?

A: Yes. Start with what you know or are curious about. Skills grow with action and learning. Freelancing, content creation, and small digital products are great starting points.

Q2: How much time do I need to dedicate daily?

A: Even 1 hour/day consistently is enough to get started. As you grow, you can scale your efforts.

Q3: How do I manage side hustles with a full-time job?

A: Time-blocking is essential. Treat side hustles like mini-businesses: plan weekly tasks, prioritize revenue-generating actions, and automate repetitive tasks.

Q4: I'm scared of losing money. What should I do?

A: Start small. Focus on low-risk, calculated steps. Treat failures as learning experiences, not setbacks.

Q5: When will I see results?

A: Results vary. Small wins usually appear in weeks, bigger income streams grow over months. Patience, consistency, and reinvestment compound results.

Q6: Can this really lead to financial independence?

A: Yes, if you follow mindset shifts, side hustle strategies, reinvestment principles, and habits consistently. Freedom grows gradually but sustainably.

23

Discover Your Skills & Passions

"You've always dreamed of earning more, but the 9-to-5 routine keeps you stuck. What if the skill you already have could become your first side hustle?"

Why this chapter matters

Before you earn your first extra ₹10k, you need clarity. Most people jump into side hustles blindly—copying what others do. That's why this chapter focuses on **you**: your skills, your passions, and your experiences.

Step 1: Identify What You're Good At

Ask yourself:

- What tasks do I do that others often ask me to help with?
- Which skills have I picked up through work, hobbies, or personal life?
- What comes naturally to me that I could teach, sell, or monetize?

Example from my journey:

When I first started, I realized I was good at **breaking complex digital**

marketing ideas into simple steps. People often messaged me asking how I created funnels or grew a social media page. That skill became my **first monetizable side hustle**.

Exercise:
Write down **5 skills or talents** you have that others might pay for. Don't overthink—just list everything.

Step 2: What Do You Enjoy Doing?

Side hustles succeed when they combine **skill + passion**. Ask yourself:

- What tasks make me lose track of time?
- What subjects do I enjoy learning about or talking about?
- If money wasn't a concern, what would I do every day?

I started my first freelance projects not because I was desperate for money, but because I genuinely loved teaching and sharing my knowledge. Passion fuels consistency, and consistency fuels income.

Exercise:
Circle **3 activities you enjoy** the most and write how you could potentially monetize them.

Step 3: Explore Market Demand

It's not enough to be good at something; people must **pay for it**.

- Check online marketplaces: Fiverr, Upwork, Etsy, or local Facebook groups.
- Ask friends or colleagues: Would they pay for this service?
- Look for gaps: Where is demand higher than supply?

Mini story:

One of my early experiments: I offered **simple Canva designs for small businesses**. I barely knew Canva, but businesses were paying ₹500–₹1000 per design. I realized the demand was there; I just needed to package my skill.

Exercise:

Pick **one skill** from Step 1 + one passion from Step 2. Search online and offline to validate if people will pay for it. Note at least **3 ways to monetize it**.

Step 4: Your Unique Angle

Even if multiple people offer similar services, your **experience, personality, or method** makes you unique. Ask yourself:

- How can I solve a problem faster, easier, or cheaper?
- Can I combine two skills into one offer?
- What's my story that makes people trust me?

Example:

I combined my digital marketing knowledge with a **step-by-step explanation style** for beginners. Instead of generic advice, I created templates, checklists, and examples. People loved it—and paid for it.

Exercise:

Write a **unique selling proposition (USP)** in one sentence for your side hustle idea.

Step 5: Your First Micro Offer

You don't need a full-fledged business to start. Begin with a **micro offer**—something small you can deliver in 1–3 hours.

- Examples: a one-hour coaching call, a digital template, a mini-design, or a small batch product.
- Price it to reflect value but keep it approachable for first buyers.

My first micro offer earned ₹1,500. It was small money, but the **confidence and experience** I gained were priceless. That first win fueled me to scale.

Exercise:

Create **one micro offer** you can deliver this week. List what you'll sell, who will buy, and how much you'll charge.

Key Takeaways

1. Identify skills you already have that can be monetized.
2. Pair skills with passion for sustainable motivation.
3. Validate demand before spending months building a product.
4. Find your unique angle—your personal story or method is valuable.
5. Start small with a micro offer; experience matters more than perfection.

Action Checklist (for this week)

- List 5 monetizable skills.
- Circle 3 passions you enjoy daily.
- Validate 1 skill + passion combination online/offline.
- Write a one-line USP for your side hustle.
- Create your first micro offer with price & delivery plan.

Your First Side Hustle – From Idea to Action

"Most people have ideas, but ideas without action are just dreams. Today, you'll learn how to turn your skill or passion into your **first real side hustle**—even if you only have 1 hour a day."

Step 1: Narrow Down Your Idea

By now, you've listed skills and passions from Chapter 1. The next step is **choosing one side hustle to focus on**.

Ask yourself:

- Which skill can I start offering this week?
- Which idea excites me enough to dedicate consistent time?
- Which idea has market demand?

I remember when I had three potential side hustles: writing blog posts, creating small digital courses, and designing social media graphics. I chose social media graphics first because I could start immediately with simple tools like Canva. That first "quick win" gave me confidence to expand later.

Exercise:

Write down the **top 3 side hustle ideas** from your skills + passion list and select **one to start this month**.

Step 2: Start Small, Deliver Fast

Many beginners get stuck trying to perfect their product before launching. That's a trap.

- Deliver a minimum viable offer (MVO) first.
- Don't wait for the "perfect" logo, website, or ad copy.
- Start selling what you can do well enough today.

I launched my first Canva design gig with **only 5 templates**. People didn't care about perfection; they cared about **results and speed.** That small launch gave me early clients and feedback to improve.

Exercise:

List **3 deliverables** you can provide in your first micro-offer. Set a **deadline this week** to deliver to at least 1 paying customer or beta tester.

Step 3: Set Your Price & Test the Market

Pricing can feel tricky. Here's a simple approach for beginners:

- Research similar offers online.
- Pick a price that reflects value but feels accessible to early buyers.
- Offer introductory discounts if needed to get first testimonials.

I priced my first digital marketing template at ₹500. It felt low compared to my effort, but that first sale gave me confidence—and the testimonial helped me raise prices to ₹1,500 in the next month.

Exercise:

Decide **one price point** for your first side hustle offer. Write it down and commit to **selling at least once** at this price this month.

Step 4: Find Your First Customers

Where do you find people willing to pay? Some beginner-friendly methods:

- Social media: Instagram, LinkedIn, Facebook groups
- Friends, family, colleagues
- Freelance marketplaces: Fiverr, Upwork, or local WhatsApp communities

My first client came from a **WhatsApp forward** I sent to 10 friends. One person shared it with a small business owner, and boom—my first ₹1,500 sale. I learned that action beats waiting for "perfect marketing."

Exercise:

Identify **3 places or people** to approach this week to sell your first offer. Draft a short, friendly message introducing your service.

Step 5: Deliver & Collect Feedback

After your first sale:

- Deliver on time, exceed expectations if possible
- Ask for feedback/testimonial
- Use feedback to improve your offer for next clients

I asked my first client: "What worked well? What could be better?" That 10-minute chat helped me refine my template and increase my next client's price by 50%. Small feedback loops **accelerate growth**.

Exercise:

After delivering your first offer, write **3 improvement points** based on feedback. Plan how to apply them to your next sale.

Key Takeaways

- Choose one side hustle idea from your skills and passions.
- Launch a minimum viable offer—don't wait for perfection.
- Price your offer reasonably and start selling immediately.
- Find first customers in your personal network or beginner-friendly marketplaces.
- Collect feedback, improve, and iterate to scale.

Action Checklist (for this week)

- Select one side hustle idea to start this month
- Identify 3 deliverables for your first offer
- Decide your first price point
- Approach 3 potential clients or platforms
- Deliver first offer and collect **feedback/testimonial**

24

Scaling Your First Side Hustle – From ₹1k to ₹10k per Month

"You've made your first sale—congratulations! But here's the real test: turning that one-time win into a **consistent ₹10k/month income**. Scaling isn't magic—it's a simple, repeatable system."

Step 1: Track Your Metrics

Scaling starts with clarity. You need to know:

- How much are you earning per client or product?
- How many clients or sales can you realistically serve per week?
- Where are your highest-paying opportunities?

When I scaled my first freelance side hustle, I realized I was spending hours on low-paying clients. By tracking metrics, I shifted focus to **high-value clients**, doubling revenue without working more hours.

Exercise:

Create a simple **tracking sheet** (Excel, Google Sheets, or notebook):
| Client/Product | Price | Hours Spent | Profit | Notes |
Track your first 5 clients or sales. Identify where you spend the most

time vs. profit.

Step 2: Raise Your Prices Strategically

Beginners hesitate to increase prices, but **value grows faster than effort**. Ask yourself:

- How can I improve my offer without significantly increasing my workload?
- Can I package multiple services/products together for higher value?
- Are testimonials available to justify higher pricing?

My first Canva gig was ₹500 per design. After 10 sales, I bundled **5 designs + template edits** and charged ₹2,500. Clients loved the value, and my monthly income jumped without adding extra hours.

Exercise:

List **3 ways** to increase the value of your offer so you can raise your price this month.

Step 3: Automate & Streamline Repetitive Tasks

You can only scale if you **save time on repetitive tasks**. Examples:

- Pre-made templates for your service
- Standardized client onboarding messages
- Quick delivery systems using free tools

I created a **template library** for my first digital product. Suddenly, I could deliver multiple projects a day without extra effort, freeing time to find new clients.

Exercise:

Identify **2 tasks you repeat** in your side hustle. Write down how to automate or streamline them this month.

Step 4: Expand Your Client Base

Scaling requires **more buyers**. Start small and strategic:

- Reach out to networks: LinkedIn, WhatsApp, Facebook groups
- Partner with someone who has your target audience
- Ask existing clients for referrals

I emailed 10 previous clients asking for referrals. 3 responded with leads, and 2 became paying clients. Referrals were my **fastest route to scaling**.

Exercise:
List **5 potential referral sources** or communities where you can find new clients. Plan **one outreach action** for this week.

Step 5: Offer Packages & Upsells

Once your micro offer works, you can create **mid-tier and high-tier offers**:

- Micro offer: ₹500–₹1,000 (your first product/service)
- Mid-tier: ₹2,000–₹5,000 (bundle multiple services or provide additional features)
- High-tier: ₹10,000+ (premium, done-for-you package or coaching session)

I created a **3-tier system** for my side hustle: basic templates, complete branding kits, and mini-consulting. Even a few high-tier clients pushed me past ₹10k/month quickly.

Exercise:
Draft **2–3 tiered offers** for your side hustle. Note deliverables and pricing.

Step 6: Mindset & Consistency

Scaling is as much mindset as strategy:

- Treat your side hustle as **real business**, not a hobby.
- Focus on **consistency**, not overnight results.
- Celebrate **small milestones** to maintain momentum.

After my first ₹1,500 sale, I set a goal: **₹10k/month within 90 days**. By taking consistent steps, raising prices, and streamlining tasks, I hit that target in under 3 months. The confidence was life-changing.

Exercise:
Write your **next 90-day revenue goal**. Break it into **weekly targets**.

Key Takeaways

1. Track metrics to know where to focus energy for highest profit.
2. Raise prices strategically and increase value without overworking.
3. Automate repetitive tasks to free time for client acquisition.
4. Expand client base via networks and referrals.
5. Offer tiered packages and upsells to increase monthly revenue.
6. Maintain mindset, consistency, and celebrate milestones.

Action Checklist (for this week)

- Track first 5 client sales or orders with metrics
- Identify 3 ways to **raise your offer's value**
- Automate or streamline 2 repetitive tasks
- List 5 sources to expand your client base
- Draft 2–3 tiered offers with pricing
- Set 90-day revenue goal and weekly targets

Money Mindset & Reinvesting – Turning Side Hustles into Real Wealth

"Making money is the first step—but keeping it, multiplying it, and growing it is where **real wealth begins**. Most people earn, spend, and repeat. Today, you'll learn to **break that cycle**."

Step 1: Understand the Money Mindset Gap

Middle-class earners often follow the same pattern:

- Earn → Spend → Regret → Repeat
- This mindset keeps you trapped in the **'paycheck-to-paycheck' cycle**.

Mindset shift:
Think like a **builder, not just an earner**. Every rupee you earn can be:

- Saved strategically
- Reinvested into your side hustle
- Used to create new income streams

I used to reinvest just a tiny portion of my earnings. Once I committed **50% of profits from side hustles back into learning and tools**, my income multiplied in months. That reinvestment mindset changed everything.

Exercise:
Track your last month's income. Write down **how much you saved, reinvested, and spent**. Identify **one area to reinvest more** this month.

Step 2: Budget Like a Wealth Builder

Budgeting isn't about restriction—it's about **control and direction**.

Simple framework:

1. 50% for essentials (living expenses)
2. 30% for reinvestment (tools, marketing, courses)
3. 20% for personal savings or investments

When I first followed this model, I realized I was spending more than necessary on things that didn't grow my income. Shifting just 30% into side hustle reinvestment gave me **better tools, faster results, and bigger clients**.

Exercise:

Create your **first wealth-building budget** for this month using the 50/30/20 rule.

Step 3: Reinvest into Your Side Hustle

Reinvesting means using a portion of earnings to **expand your capacity or value**:

- Upgrade software/tools to save time
- Take a short course to learn new skills
- Outsource small tasks to focus on high-value work

I invested ₹5,000 in a Canva course. Within 2 months, I charged ₹2,500 per client instead of ₹500, and my first 10k+ month followed. Small reinvestments lead to **compound growth**.

Exercise:

Identify **one area of your side hustle** where reinvestment could increase income. Allocate **a specific amount** this month.

Step 4: Save with Purpose

Saving isn't just stashing cash—it's preparing for opportunities:

- Emergency fund: 3–6 months of essential expenses
- Opportunity fund: for new ventures or side hustle expansion
- Investment fund: for stocks, mutual funds, or other assets

I built a small "opportunity fund" from my first ₹10k income. That fund allowed me to **launch my next side hustle without financial stress**, accelerating growth and confidence.

Exercise:

Open 3 virtual "envelopes" for savings: emergency, opportunity, investment. Decide **how much to allocate** from your next side hustle income.

Step 5: Mindset Around Risk & Reinvestment

Many people fear losing money and avoid reinvestment. Real growth comes from **calculated risk**:

- Test small investments first
- Track ROI (return on investment)
- Scale only when the result is proven

I reinvested a small portion of my first side hustle income into Fiverr ads. The first month returned **3x my investment**. Seeing small wins reduced my fear and encouraged **bigger, smarter bets**.

Exercise:

Identify **one small reinvestment risk** you can take this month and set a **success metric** to measure ROI.

Step 6: Compound Your Earnings

The magic of reinvesting is **compounding**: small improvements accumulate:

- ₹1,000 invested in learning this month → ₹2,500 next month → ₹5,000 in 3 months
- Reinvested profits multiply faster than additional effort alone

By continuously reinvesting, I grew my side hustle from ₹1k/month to ₹25k/month in 6 months. Compounding works faster than working harder—it's the **millionaire mindset in action**.

Exercise:
Write down **3 ways to reinvest earnings** from your side hustle to compound growth over the next 3 months.

Key Takeaways

1. Shift your mindset: earn, save, and reinvest strategically.
2. Budget like a builder: control, don't restrict.
3. Reinvest profits to grow skills, tools, or reach.
4. Save with purpose: emergency, opportunity, and investment funds.
5. Take calculated reinvestment risks to accelerate growth.
6. Leverage compounding for long-term wealth.

Action Checklist (for this week)

- Track income, spending, and reinvestment
- Create your 50/30/20 wealth-building budget
- Identify one reinvestment opportunity in your side hustle

- Allocate savings into 3 purpose-driven envelopes
- Identify one small reinvestment risk to test this month
- Plan 3 ways to compound earnings over the next 3 months

25

Scaling Your Hustle

Many beginners stop after their first ₹10,000. They feel proud, but then stuck. Why? Because they don't know how to *scale.*

Scaling means building systems that allow you to earn **more money without increasing effort in the same proportion.**

Think of it like this:

- A chaiwala sells 50 cups a day, working 12 hours. That's effort.
- A café owner sets up two outlets, hires staff, and sells 500 cups. That's scale.

Your hustle needs the same transformation.

1. From Hustler to Builder

In the beginning, you're doing everything yourself. That's normal. But scaling means shifting identity:

- From **hustler** (one-person army) → to **builder** (someone who creates processes, assets, and systems).

Ask yourself:

- Am I still exchanging only time for money?
- Can I create something once and sell it multiple times?
- Can I leverage other people, tools, or platforms to multiply output?

Scaling is not about working harder; it's about working smarter.

2. Three Paths to Scaling a Hustle

Path A: Increase Prices

Once you've proven your skill or product, raise your rates.

- A freelancer charging ₹500 per article can move to ₹1,500 once they have 5 testimonials.
- A tutor teaching at ₹200/hour can shift to ₹500/hour after showing results.

Confidence from small wins gives you the right to charge more.

Path B: Increase Volume

If you're selling products, increase sales volume.

- Sell on multiple platforms (Amazon, Flipkart, Instagram).
- Automate outreach (use tools to send bulk messages, run ads, or list in more marketplaces).

Case: Raj started selling handmade candles on Instagram. After 50 sales, he scaled by listing on Amazon and Myntra. In 3 months, his sales jumped 10x without 10x effort.

Path C: Create Systems & Assets

This is where real growth happens. Build things that keep working:

- **Digital Products** – E-books, templates, recorded courses (created once, sold unlimited times).
- **Teams** – Hire freelancers for design, writing, or customer service.
- **Automation** – Use tools (email sequences, chatbots, ads) to reach 1000 people while you sleep.

This is where your hustle shifts from **self-employed** to **entrepreneurship**.

3. The Scaling Pyramid

Visualize a pyramid:

Base Layer – Small Wins (₹1k–₹10k)

✅ Freelancing, small sales, testing ideas

Middle Layer – Consistency (₹10k–₹50k)

✅ Building client base, repeat customers, increasing efficiency

Top Layer – Scaling (₹50k–₹5L+)

✅ Systems, automation, digital products, teams, brand building

You can't jump to the top without climbing the base and middle. Each layer strengthens the next.

4. Mistakes Beginners Make While Scaling

1. **Scaling too early** – Hiring staff or running ads before proof of concept.
2. **Not documenting processes** – Doing things randomly instead of creating repeatable systems.
3. **Focusing only on sales, not delivery** – Growth collapses if quality drops.
4. **Burnout** – Trying to scale by working harder, not smarter.

Remember: scaling should *reduce* stress, not increase it.

5. Exercise – Scaling Roadmap

Grab your journal and answer these:

1. What's one part of my hustle I can **charge more for**?
2. What's one way I can **increase volume** without doubling my effort?
3. What system/asset/tool can I build today that will pay me repeatedly?

Example:

- Charge ₹2,000 per project instead of ₹1,000.
- Upload product on Amazon in addition to Instagram.
- Record a 1-hour workshop once, and sell it for ₹499 every month.

6. Story: How Vivek Scaled from ₹10k to ₹1L/month

Vivek started as a freelance video editor charging ₹1,000 per video. In 3 months, he had 10 clients and no time left. He almost burned out.

Then he did three things:

- Raised his price to ₹3,000 per video.
- Hired a junior editor at ₹15,000/month to help.
- Started offering a "monthly package" of 10 videos for ₹25,000.

Within 6 months, Vivek was making ₹1 lakh/month, but working fewer hours than before.

Lesson: Scaling is not magic—it's about strategy.

7. Mentor's Tip: The 70-20-10 Rule for Scaling

- **70%** of effort = What already works (keep doing it).
- **20%** = Improving existing systems (hire, automate, streamline).
- **10%** = Experimenting with new opportunities.

This keeps growth steady while avoiding chaos.

Section 8: Real Case Studies of Scaling

Case Study 1: Freelancing – Meera's Design Hustle

Meera, a full-time college student, began with logo design on Fiverr. Her first gig was ₹700. She did 10 small projects and gained 5-star reviews.

Instead of staying stuck at low prices, she:

1. Created 3 service packages – Basic, Standard, Premium.
2. Increased rates gradually (₹700 → ₹1,500 → ₹3,000 per logo).
3. Added one junior designer for background work.

Result: Within 8 months, she was earning **₹70,000/month part-time**, and her side hustle became her main income.

Lesson: Create *packages*, not one-off services. This gives clients choice and lets you scale revenue.

Case Study 2: Content Creation – Arjun's Instagram Growth

Arjun loved fitness and started posting short reels. His first milestone was 1,000 followers. At that stage, he could not monetize much.

To scale, he:

1. Launched an eBook on "Home Workouts Without Equipment" priced at ₹299.

2. Ran collaborations with 3 micro-influencers (low cost but high trust).
3. Started offering online group classes.

Within 1 year, he scaled to **₹1.2L per month** from products + coaching.

Lesson: Scaling for creators = Products + Partnerships.

Case Study 3: E-Commerce – Priya's Handmade Jewelry

Priya sold handmade jewelry on Instagram, but packaging and shipping ate all her time.

To scale, she:

1. Partnered with a local packaging vendor.
2. Outsourced shipping to Shiprocket.
3. Expanded listings to Amazon & Meesho.

Result: Her orders grew 5x while her workload decreased.

Lesson: Use platforms and logistics partners—don't do everything yourself.

Section 9: Scaling Framework – The 3X Rule

Before you scale, ask yourself these 3X questions:

1. **Can I triple my output without triple effort?**

- If no → find automation or outsourcing.

1. **Can I triple my prices with better packaging?**

- If yes → focus on value-based positioning.

1. **Can I triple my reach with the same product/service?**

- If yes → expand to more platforms, ads, or affiliates.

Scaling is always about leverage, never about brute force.

Section 10: Mentor's Scaling Checklist

Use this checklist to track your hustle growth:

- I have proof of concept (at least 5–10 paying clients/customers).
- I've raised my prices at least once.
- I've automated or outsourced one small task.
- I have one repeatable system (email sequence, marketplace listing, package offer).
- I've documented my delivery process (so someone else could do it).

Section 11: Reflection & Worksheet

Worksheet: My Scaling Roadmap

1. My current hustle: ______________________________
2. My current monthly income: _____________________
3. My next target (3 months): ______________________

Part A: Increase Prices

- Current price: ________
- New price (next 3 clients): ________

Part B: Increase Volume

- Current platform(s): ________
- New platform I will test: ________

Part C: Systems & Assets

- Task I can outsource: ________
- Asset I can create once and sell multiple times: ________

Write your answers now. Don't just read. Execution = Scaling.

Section 12: Mentor's Note – Scaling ≠ Greed

A caution: Scaling is not about showing off income screenshots. It's about *creating breathing space.*

- At ₹10k/month, you pay bills.
- At ₹50k/month, you buy comfort.
- At ₹1L/month, you buy freedom.

But remember: **freedom comes only if you scale smartly, not if you burn out.**

Section 13: Additional Inspiration – Global Scaling Stories

- **Shopify Dropshipping** – A college student in Canada scaled from $500 to $50,000/month by automating suppliers.
- **Udemy Instructor** – A teacher in India recorded one coding course, which now sells globally while he sleeps.
- **Affiliate Blogger** – A homemaker in Kerala started a recipe blog. After 12 months, she earned ₹80k/month from affiliate cooking products.

Lesson: Scaling = finding leverage points unique to your hustle.

Section 14: Mini-Exercise – Write Your "Scaling Statement"

Write one bold sentence about your next move:

"In the next 90 days, I will scale my side hustle from ₹____ to ₹____ by [raising prices / outsourcing / creating an asset]."

Put it on a sticky note, paste it on your wall, and revisit daily.

26

Understanding Market Needs – Finding Opportunities People Will Pay For

You can have the best skills or the flashiest ideas—but if no one wants to pay for them, your side hustle won't survive. Understanding the market is the **fastest way to make your first ₹10k and beyond**."

Step 1: Spot the Real Demand

Most beginners assume:

"I'll create something I like, and people will buy it."

Reality: **people pay for solutions, not passions**. Your job is to **discover unmet needs**.

When I started my first digital design service, I initially targeted a general audience. No one bought. Then I realized **small business owners needed branded Instagram posts** but didn't know where to get them. I focused on that niche, and my first ₹5k sale came within a week.

Exercise:

Write down **5 problems people around you face**. Ask: "Would they pay for a solution?"

Step 2: Research & Validate Demand

Before investing time or money, validate that people **actually want to pay**:

- Check Google Trends for related searches
- Join Facebook or WhatsApp groups and observe conversations
- Look at competitors: what are they offering and at what price?

I noticed small businesses frequently complained about **DIY Instagram templates being time-consuming**. That pain point became my first product idea, validated by 3 early clients before I fully invested.

Exercise:
Pick one idea and **check 3 sources**: online search trends, social media groups, and competitor offerings. Confirm **real interest exists**.

Step 3: Identify Overlooked Niches

High demand often hides in **small, overlooked areas**:

- Industries that are underserved
- Specific problems within a large market
- Emerging trends or untapped audiences

Instead of offering generic Canva designs, I focused on **restaurant menus and social media kits** a niche many ignored. This made me the "go-to expert" and allowed me to **charge premium pricing**.

Exercise:
List **3 niche opportunities** in your skill area that are being overlooked. Highlight which one excites you most.

Step 4: Test Your Offer Quickly

Instead of spending months perfecting a product:

- Offer a **minimum viable solution**
- Pre-sell or take early orders
- Gather feedback to improve

I offered my first Instagram template bundle to 5 small business owners via direct message. 3 bought immediately. Their feedback allowed me to **refine and upsell** my next batch.

Exercise:
Write down **1 small test offer** you can launch this week. Identify **2–3 people** who might buy it.

Step 5: Price for Market, Not Ego

Many beginners undervalue their work:

- Price too low → perceived as cheap or amateur
- Price too high → scare off first buyers

I initially charged ₹200 per design. After testing value-based pricing, I raised it to ₹500–₹700. People paid happily because it **solved their problem and saved time**.

Exercise:
Determine **your first 3 price points**: micro, mid, and premium. Base it on **value delivered, not hours spent**.

Step 6: Observe & Iterate

Market needs are dynamic. Keep observing:

- Feedback from clients
- Social media trends
- New tools or competitors

After my first side hustle success, I noticed clients wanted **ready-to-use Instagram campaigns**, not just templates. I pivoted, creating packages that sold 3x faster.

Exercise:
Set a **weekly 30-minute review** to note market feedback and spot trends. Ask: "What can I tweak or offer next?"

Key Takeaways

1. People pay for solutions, not hobbies.
2. Validate demand before investing heavily.
3. Small, overlooked niches often hold high-value opportunities.
4. Test offers quickly and gather feedback.
5. Price strategically, based on value, not ego.
6. Observe, iterate, and stay aligned with market needs.

Action Checklist (for this week)

- List 5 problems people around you face that could be solved
- Validate one idea using search trends, social media groups, or competitors
- Identify 3 overlooked niches in your skill area
- Launch a small test offer with 2–3 potential buyers
- Set your first micro, mid, and premium price points

- Schedule a weekly 30-minute market review

Choosing Your First Side Hustle – Turning Ideas into Action

You don't need a perfect plan or endless resources to start. You need clarity, courage, and a first step. Today, we'll pick **your first side hustle** and map out the first 30 days to make it real."

Step 1: Know Your Options

Most beginners get stuck thinking:
"I have to invent something unique or revolutionary."
Truth: the simplest hustles often work best. Common side hustles include:

1. **Freelancing:** Sell your skills—writing, designing, coding, marketing.
2. **Content Creation:** YouTube, blogs, Instagram, or TikTok—monetize via ads, affiliate marketing, or sponsorships.
3. **Digital Products:** Templates, ebooks, courses, tools, printables.
4. **Small Businesses:** Dropshipping, reselling, niche services, or consulting.

Mini-case story:

- Ramesh, a college graduate, started offering **social media post designs** on Fiverr. First ₹10k earned in 2 weeks.
- Priya, a housewife, created a **budget planner template** and sold it on Etsy, earning ₹12k in a month.
- Akash, a software engineer, started a small **local web design service**, making ₹15k in the first month.

Exercise:

Write down **3 side hustle ideas** from the above list that fit your skills and interests.

Step 2: Match Skills with Market Needs

Your side hustle should solve a **real problem**:

- Freelance skills: Can someone pay for your design, writing, or coding skill?
- Digital products: Does it save time, teach something, or entertain?
- Small business: Is there local or online demand you can fulfill?

I started my first side hustle by **looking at what people paid for around me**. I had no perfect skill set, but I **matched my beginner-level skills with real demand**. That approach helped me earn my first ₹10k without wasting months experimenting.

Exercise:

For each of your 3 ideas, **write 1 problem it solves** and **how someone benefits from it**.

Step 3: Assess Your Time & Resources

Side hustles should fit your **current life situation**:

- How many hours per day can you realistically dedicate?
- What tools, platforms, or budget do you have?
- Can you leverage free resources initially?

I only had 1–2 hours a day after my job, so I focused on small, fast-turnaround freelance tasks. It wasn't glamorous, but it **built confidence, skill, and cash flow**.

Exercise:

Write down **how much time you can commit daily or weekly** for your side hustle. Match this with the type of hustle from Step 1.

Step 4: Start Small & Test

Don't overcomplicate. Start with:

- Minimum viable offer
- One platform (Fiverr, Instagram, Etsy, local network)
- Goal: first ₹1k–₹10k revenue

Mini-case study:

Neha, a graphic design beginner, offered **Instagram post templates** to 5 clients first. She earned ₹7k in the first 3 weeks. That small success motivated her to scale.

Exercise:

Pick **one test offer** for your first side hustle. Note: pricing, delivery method, and target audience.

Step 5: 30-Day Action Plan

Your first month should focus on **learning, testing, and earning**. Suggested plan:

- **Week 1:** Research, define target audience, and finalize offer
- **Week 2:** Set up your profile, product, or service page
- **Week 3:** Reach out to 5–10 potential clients/customers
- **Week 4:** Deliver work, collect feedback, and reinvest earnings

Exercise:

Create your **personal 30-day action plan** for your first side hustle, including specific tasks and deadlines.

Key Takeaways

1. Pick a side hustle that **matches your skills and market demand**.
2. Start small, focus on **quick wins**.
3. Assess your time and resources realistically.
4. Offer a **minimum viable solution** first.
5. Use a **30-day plan** to gain momentum and confidence.

Action Checklist (for this week)

- List 3 potential side hustles aligned with your skills and interests
- Define **the problem each hustle solves**
- Assess how much time and resources you can dedicate
- Choose **one side hustle to start this month**
- Draft a 30-day action plan with weekly tasks

27

Setting Realistic Goals & Milestones – Your First Wins Matter

Big dreams can feel overwhelming. But achieving your **first ₹10k or first client** is what turns ambition into reality. Today, we focus on **micro-goals** that build momentum and confidence."

Step 1: Why Micro-Goals Matter

Many beginners set vague goals:

"I want to make money from a side hustle."

Without measurable steps, it rarely happens. Micro-goals help you:

- Track progress
- Stay motivated
- Celebrate small wins

When I started freelancing, my first goal wasn't ₹1 lakh per month. It was **getting my first 3 clients in 30 days**. Achieving this small milestone gave me confidence to scale fast.

Exercise:

Write down **one small goal** you can realistically achieve in the next week related to your side hustle.

Step 2: Identify Key Milestones

Micro-goals should be **specific, measurable, and achievable**. Examples:

1. First ₹10k earned
2. First client or sale
3. Launch first product/service

Mini-case study:

- Ramesh, a first-time freelancer, set a milestone: **3 completed orders in 30 days**. He hit it and earned ₹12k.
- Priya, selling printables, set her milestone: **50 template downloads**. This early success motivated her to **create more products**.

Exercise:
List **3 micro-goals** you aim to achieve in the next 30 days. Include what success looks like for each.

Step 3: Break Milestones into Actionable Steps

Each milestone should have clear **steps you can execute daily or weekly**:

- Reach out to potential clients
- Set up a product page
- Promote on social media
- Deliver work and collect feedback

I used a simple daily checklist to track **outreach, delivery, and follow-ups**. Seeing progress each day kept me motivated and prevented procrastination.

Exercise:

Break each micro-goal into **3–5 actionable steps** you can complete this week.

Step 4: Track Your Progress & Adjust

Regularly review:

- Did you complete the steps?
- Are you on track for your milestones?
- What obstacles need adjustment?

In my first freelancing month, one milestone was **5 inquiries sent per day**. By tracking, I realized I needed **better messaging**. Adjusting the approach increased client responses by 60%.

Exercise:

Set a **weekly review time** (30 minutes) to assess your milestones and adjust your plan.

Step 5: Celebrate Small Wins

Every small win compounds motivation:

- First ₹1k earned → confidence boost
- First positive client feedback → credibility boost
- First product launch → mindset shift

Mini-case study:

Akash, a small business beginner, celebrated **his first ₹10k month** with a small personal reward. That emotional reward reinforced his commitment to **scale further**.

Exercise:

Decide **one small reward** for achieving your first micro-goal this month.

Key Takeaways

1. Micro-goals turn big dreams into achievable steps.
2. Set 3 specific milestones for your first 30 days.
3. Break milestones into actionable daily/weekly tasks.
4. Track progress and adjust when needed.
5. Celebrate small wins to build confidence and momentum.

Action Checklist (for this week)

- Write down **3 measurable milestones** for the next 30 days
- Break each milestone into **3–5 actionable steps**
- Schedule a **weekly review** for progress and adjustments
- Decide on a **small reward** for achieving your first milestone

Time Management for Beginners – Make Every Hour Count

Your side hustle won't grow on its own. But just **1 focused hour a day** can change everything. Today, we learn how to balance work, family, and your dreams without burning out."

Step 1: Why Time Management Matters

Many beginners struggle because they **overestimate available time** and **underestimate effort**. Balancing a 9-to-5, family commitments, and a side hustle requires discipline and smart planning.

When I started my first side hustle, I had a full-time job. Initially, I tried working late at night and weekends, which left me exhausted. Once I created a **1-hour daily power session**, my progress skyrocketed without sacrificing sleep or family time.

Exercise:

Track your current daily schedule for 3 days. Note time spent on work, commute, chores, and leisure. Identify **1 hour you can dedicate to your side hustle** consistently.

Step 2: The 1-Hour Daily Power Session

Focus beats duration. Use this hour to:

1. Work on your highest-priority task (first client, product creation, outreach)
2. Eliminate distractions (phone notifications, TV, social media)
3. Take notes and track progress

Mini-case study:

Priya, a homemaker, dedicated **1 hour after lunch daily** to create and market her printable templates. Within a month, she earned her first ₹10k with minimal disruption to family routines.

Exercise:

Plan your **1-hour session**: time, location, and primary task. Commit it to your weekly schedule.

Step 3: Prioritize Tasks with the 80/20 Rule

Focus on the **20% of tasks that bring 80% of results**:

- Client outreach over social media scrolling
- Product creation over endless research
- Learning strategies that directly impact income

I always ask myself:

"Will this task move me closer to my first ₹10k?"

If not, it waits. This mindset **keeps side hustlers focused and productive**.

Exercise:

List all tasks you plan to do for your side hustle this week. Highlight the **3 tasks with the highest impact**.

Step 4: Combine Micro-Habits with Big Goals

Even small blocks of time add up. Use:

- **Commute time:** Listen to audiobooks or podcasts
- **Waiting periods:** Draft emails or social media posts
- **Lunch breaks:** Quick learning sessions

Ramesh, a college graduate, turned his daily 30-minute commute into **skill-building sessions**. Over two months, he gained enough confidence to start offering freelance services, earning his first ₹12k.

Exercise:

Identify **3 micro-time blocks** you can utilize this week for side hustle growth.

Step 5: Avoid Burnout

Balance is key. Tips:

- Schedule **1 rest day per week**
- Use **time-blocking** for family and personal tasks
- Celebrate small wins to stay motivated

I make Sundays a "no-side-hustle day" to recharge. This **prevents burnout** and keeps me productive on weekdays.

Exercise:

Plan your **weekly schedule** including 1 power hour per day and a rest day. Stick to it for 30 days.

Key Takeaways

1. Track your current schedule and find **1 consistent hour** for your side hustle.
2. Focus on high-impact tasks using the **80/20 rule**.
3. Use micro-time blocks throughout the day for incremental progress.
4. Avoid burnout by scheduling rest and family time.
5. Commit to your 1-hour daily power session consistently.

Mini-Checklist

- Track current schedule for 3 days
- Identify **1 hour/day** for side hustle growth
- Highlight **3 high-impact tasks** for the week
- Find **3 micro-time blocks** for incremental progress
- Schedule **rest and recharge time**

28

Building Your First Customer Base

When you start a side hustle, money doesn't come from thin air. It comes from people—customers who believe in you enough to pay for what you're offering. But here's the truth: most beginners get stuck here. They create something, sit back, and wait... only to feel disappointed when no one shows up.

I've been there. I remember building my first funnel late at night, convinced people would magically find it. Spoiler alert: they didn't. Not until I learned one golden rule—**you don't find customers, you earn them**.

Let's break it down simply, step by step.

1. Start with Trust, Not Selling

In the beginning, your biggest asset isn't your product—it's *trust*. People don't buy from strangers, they buy from someone they trust, like, and believe can help them.

- If you're freelancing: offer to do a small task for free or discounted in exchange for a testimonial.
- If you're selling products: share your story—why you created it, what

problem it solves.
- If you're teaching/coaching: give away bite-sized value first (like tips on Instagram or LinkedIn).

Think of it this way: every post, every chat, every conversation is like putting a brick in the foundation of trust.

2. Your First 10 Customers

Don't think about "hundreds of sales." Think about the **first 10 customers.**

Why? Because those first 10 become your proof, your testimonials, your momentum.

Here's a simple roadmap:

1. Write down a list of 20 people you know—friends, colleagues, old classmates.
2. Reach out personally: "Hey, I've started [your side hustle]. I'm helping [type of people] with [problem]. Do you know anyone who might benefit?"
3. Even if only 5 say yes, that's your start.

I know hustlers who made their first ₹10k just by asking their network. No ads. No website. Just courage.

3. Word of Mouth is Your Free Marketing

Middle-class people often underestimate this, but **your network is your net worth**.

When you serve your first few customers really well, they talk. And that talk is priceless—it spreads faster than any ad.

Case Study:

Ravi, a 25-year-old graphic designer, started freelancing after his 9-to-5. His first client was a friend's cousin. That one project led to three referrals, and within 3 months, Ravi was making ₹30k/month from word-of-mouth alone—no ads, no website, just good work.

4. Build Social Proof Early

People trust people. Screenshots, testimonials, reviews—these are gold.

- Share your wins (even small ones) on social media.
- Post your first ₹1,000 earned.
- Thank your first customer publicly.

Every small proof makes the next person say, "If they did it, maybe I can trust them too."

5. Don't Overcomplicate Sales

Most beginners think they need fancy funnels, websites, or logos. You don't. At the start, **sales = conversations**.

- Send a DM.
- Pick up the phone.
- Share your offer in a WhatsApp group.

That's it. Simplicity wins when you're building your base.

Exercise: Building Your First 10 Customers

1. Make a list of 20 people you know who *might* need your side hustle service/product.
2. Draft a simple message introducing what you do.
3. Commit to sending that message to all 20 people this week.
4. Write down how many responses you get.

Your goal: land your **first 3–5 paying customers** within 30 days.

Remember, building your customer base isn't about "getting lucky." It's about showing up, reaching out, and creating trust brick by brick. Do that, and soon you'll have more than a side hustle—you'll have a foundation for financial freedom.

Small Wins Build Confidence

Do you remember the first time you earned money on your own—without a salary slip or boss? That feeling of holding cash (or seeing that notification) was more than just money. It was proof. Proof that *you can do it.*

For most middle-class people, the journey to becoming financially free feels impossible because the mountain looks too big. They look at "millionaire" or "crorepati" and think, *Not me, not now.*

But here's the secret: **you don't climb Everest in one leap—you climb step by step.** And in business, those steps are called *small wins.*

1. Why Small Wins Matter More Than Big Dreams

Dreams are fuel, but wins are proof.
When you:

- Earn your first ₹1,000 from freelancing
- Sell your first e-book to a stranger online
- Get your first testimonial from a happy client

...your brain shifts. Suddenly, money outside a job isn't a fantasy—it's real.

I remember my first online win: I sold a ₹499 digital guide. It wasn't huge money, but when I saw that payment come in, I smiled like I had made ₹5 lakh. That single sale gave me more confidence than all the motivational videos I had watched before.

Because confidence doesn't come from theory—it comes from action.

2. The "Momentum Effect" of Small Wins

Psychologists call it the **progress principle**: when we feel progress, even tiny progress, our motivation skyrockets.

Think about it:

- A gym-goer who sees their first 1 kg weight loss keeps going.
- A student who scores 5 marks higher feels encouraged to study more.
- A hustler who earns their first ₹500 online starts dreaming of ₹5,000.

Each win creates momentum. Momentum creates belief. Belief creates results.

3. The First ₹10k Formula

Here's a simple way to think about your early hustle: **forget lakhs, focus on your first ₹10,000.**

- Sell 20 items at ₹500 each
- Offer 5 services at ₹2,000 each
- Get 2 coaching clients at ₹5,000 each

Doesn't sound impossible, right? Yet, many people quit before even trying. If you just aim for this small win—₹10k—you'll unlock the mindset of a builder, not just a dreamer.

Case Study:

Sneha, a college graduate, started freelance content writing. She charged just ₹500 per article. Within 2 months, she wrote 20 articles, made her first ₹10k, and built her confidence to raise prices. Today, she charges ₹2,000 per article, but that *first 10k win* was the confidence booster she needed.

4. Stack Wins Like Building Blocks

One win leads to another. Think of it like a staircase:

- First step: ₹1,000
- Next step: ₹10,000
- Next: ₹50,000
- Then: ₹1,00,000

Each step feels possible only after you've conquered the one before. Trying to jump directly to the top will only leave you frustrated. But stacking small wins creates a solid foundation.

5. Why Most People Ignore Small Wins

Here's the trap: middle-class conditioning teaches us to only value *big wins*. A "safe job," a "promotion," a "retirement plan."

But in the hustle world, if you ignore small wins, you'll never reach big ones. Imagine dismissing your first ₹500 and saying, *"It's too small."* You'd be throwing away the seed before it can grow into a tree.

The richest people in the world started small:

- Jeff Bezos sold his first book online.
- Dhirubhai Ambani started with trading yarn.
- Every freelancer starts with a single client.

They didn't wait for perfection—they valued the small wins.

6. Exercise: Your Small Wins Roadmap

Grab a notebook and write:

1. What's ONE small financial win I can achieve in the next 7 days?
2. (Example: Offer to design a poster for ₹500, sell one item, or teach one student online.)
3. What's ONE bigger win I can aim for in the next 30 days?
4. (Example: Earn first ₹10,000, get 3 new clients, or sell 20 products.)
5. Write down how you will celebrate each win. (Yes, celebration matters—it trains your brain to chase more wins!)

7. The Confidence Loop

Here's the formula:

Small Wins → Confidence → Bigger Action → Bigger Wins → Unstoppable Confidence.

Once you enter this loop, there's no stopping you. Your job may feel like "security," but your hustle will start feeling like *freedom*. And with every win, you'll trust yourself more.

Final Thought:

Don't underestimate the power of small wins. That first ₹1,000 or ₹10,000 may not change your bank balance much, but it will change *you*. And once you change, your future wealth is just a matter of time.

29

Building Multiple Streams of Hustle Income

Section 1 : Why One Stream Is Never Enough

Imagine a river flowing strongly through your village. Life depends on it—drinking water, farming, fishing. But one year, a dam is built upstream, and suddenly, your village dries up.

That's exactly what happens when your financial life depends on a *single income stream*. One company shuts down, one client leaves, one platform bans your account—suddenly, everything stops.

Middle-class families are most at risk here. They rely only on one paycheck. Hustlers are smarter—we build **multiple streams of income** so that even if one dries up, others keep flowing.

Section 2: The Core Idea – Layering Income, Not Jumping Around

Many beginners make the mistake of chasing *too many hustles at once*. The goal isn't to scatter energy—it's to **layer one stream at a time**:

1. Start with one hustle → Proof of concept (₹10k+ consistently).
2. Systemize/automate that hustle → Free your time.
3. Use freed time & money → Add your second hustle.
4. Rinse and repeat.

Think of it like building a house: You don't start three houses at once; you finish one room, then expand.

Section 3: Example Streams for Beginners

Here are common side hustle streams that layer well together:

- **Freelancing + Digital Products** – Start with freelance writing, then sell an eBook/course on writing tips.
- **Content + Affiliate Marketing** – Start with Instagram/YouTube, then add affiliate products to monetize trust.
- **Service Business + Consulting** – Start with designing websites, then offer consulting on branding.
- **Job + Investing** – Keep your 9–5 salary but invest part into mutual funds, stocks, or REITs.

Each pair feeds the other. You don't need 10 streams—just 2–3 strong ones.

Section 4: Case Studies – How Others Layered Streams

Case Study 1 – Rahul, the Freelancer

Rahul started with copywriting gigs on Fiverr. After 6 months:

- Income: ₹50k/month (services).
- Next step: He bundled his best sales emails into an eBook priced at ₹499.
- Within 3 months, he added ₹20k/month passive income from eBook sales.

One skill → Two streams (service + product).

Case Study 2 – Neha, the Content Creator

Neha started posting cooking reels on Instagram for fun. At 10k followers:

- Income: 0.
- She added brand collaborations (₹25k/month).
- Then launched her recipe eBook (₹299).
- Later, she started a paid cooking class (₹999).

Content → Brand deals + Products + Coaching = 3 streams.

Case Study 3 – Amit, the Job Holder

Amit kept his IT job (₹70k/month). But instead of spending, he invested:

- ₹15k/month into mutual funds.
- ₹10k/month into learning & building a small stock portfolio.
- Later, he started a blog on personal finance → ₹20k/month affiliate income.

Job security + Smart investing + Side hustle = Early independence.

Section 5: The 3 Golden Rules of Multiple Streams

1. **Don't Start All at Once** → One stream must be stable before you add another.
2. **Let Streams Feed Each Other** → Example: Freelance clients → Upsell your course.
3. **Protect from Dependency** → If one stream dies (a client, a platform), others survive.

Section 6: Mentor's Framework – 3 Levels of Hustle Income

Think of building streams in **levels**:

- **Level 1: Active Hustle Income** – Freelancing, services, side business.
- **Level 2: Semi-Passive Hustle Income** – Digital products, affiliates, small coaching.
- **Level 3: Long-Term Wealth Streams** – Investments, rentals, equity, royalties.

Don't jump to Level 3 without mastering Level 1 & 2.

Section 7: Mini-Exercise – Mapping Your Streams

Grab a paper and answer:

1. What is my **main hustle stream** right now? ____________________
2. How can I **add one related stream** in the next 3 months? ____________________
3. Which **long-term stream** can I begin small (₹1,000/month investments)? ____________________Example:

- Main Hustle = Freelance writing.
- Add Stream = Sell writing templates.

- Long-Term = Start SIP of ₹2,000/month.

Section 8: Warning – The Shiny Object Trap

Many hustlers fail because they keep chasing "the next big thing"—crypto today, dropshipping tomorrow, then quitting altogether.

The truth: Multiple streams don't mean "chasing everything." It means **mastering one, then stacking others carefully.**

Section 9: Reflection Worksheet – My 2-Year Income Map

Stream Current Status Target in 6 Months Target in 2 Years

Primary Hustle (Freelance/Service) ₹________ ₹________ ₹ ________

Secondary Hustle (Product/Coaching) ₹________ ₹________ ₹________

Wealth Stream (Investing) ₹________ ₹________ ₹________

Fill this and review monthly.

Section 10: Mentor's Note – Multiple Streams = Multiple Choices

When you depend on one income, you take whatever comes. But when you have 3–4 streams, you get the power of **choice**—the power to say no.

That's true freedom. Not just money, but independence.

Wrap-Up

- One stream = Risk.
- Multiple streams = Security + Freedom.
- Start small, stabilize, then add.
- Use your hustle to buy time, and your time to build more streams.

Section 1: When One Stream Dries Up

I'll tell you a story.

A few years back, one of my friends, Arjun, was a star freelancer. He was making over ₹1 lakh per month writing ad copy. Everyone in our group admired him—"Arjun has cracked the code," we'd say.

But then, his top two clients cut budgets in the same month. His income fell from ₹1,00,000 to just ₹25,000 overnight. The problem wasn't his skill. The problem was **dependency on one stream**.

That's when I realized: a real wealth-builder doesn't rely on a single tap. He builds an entire **pipeline system**—so even if one tap runs dry, water keeps flowing.

Middle-class people usually rely only on one salary. Hustlers build **multiple streams of income** to create *unshakable security*.

Section 2: The Trap of "One Good Job"

- The middle-class dream: "If I get one good job, I'll be set for life."
- Reality: Layoffs, inflation, automation, and company politics can cut that "dream" in a second.
- Lesson: A single stream is never enough in today's world.

Think of money as electricity. Would you power your entire house with **just one plug**? If it trips, everything dies. Multiple streams = backup generators.

Section 3: The Layering Formula

Here's my simple formula for building streams without chaos:

1. **Stream 1: Build & Stabilize** – Get one hustle to consistent ₹10k–₹20k/month.
2. **Stream 2: Systemize & Scale** – Automate/ delegate parts of it.
3. **Stream 3: Stack & Expand** – Add a related stream that feeds off the first.

Don't plant 5 seeds at once. Plant 1, water it, let it grow, then use its shade to plant the next.

Section 4: Beginner-Friendly Hustle Streams

Here's how beginners can mix & match streams:

Freelancing + Templates

- Service: Graphic design.
- Add: Sell Canva templates.

Content + Affiliate Products

- Free: YouTube channel.
- Add: Affiliate tools.

Job + Investing

- Job: Salary.
- Add: Mutual funds, SIPs, or stocks.

Small Business + Consulting

- Start: Local bakery.
- Add: Teach other bakers marketing.

Notice the pattern: **Each new stream grows naturally from the old one.**

Section 5: Deep-Dive Case Studies

Case Study 1 – Arjun the Copywriter

- Stream 1: Freelance copywriting.
- Stream 2: Created a ₹499 "Copy Template Kit."
- Stream 3: Started YouTube channel teaching copy → affiliate income.
- Result: Went from ₹1L/month unstable → ₹1.5L/month diversified.

Lesson: His streams were **stacked, not scattered**.

Case Study 2 – Sneha the Homemaker

- Stream 1: Started selling homemade pickles on Instagram.
- Stream 2: Launched a ₹299 "Pickle Recipe PDF."
- Stream 3: Affiliate for kitchen tools she used.

- Result: ₹20k/month passive on top of ₹40k product sales.

Lesson: She turned passion → product → promotion → multiple flows.

Case Study 3 – Amit the IT Guy

- Stream 1: 9–5 salary (₹70k).
- Stream 2: ₹15k/month SIPs in mutual funds.
- Stream 3: Blog on investing → affiliate links → ₹20k/month.
- Stream 4: Online investing workshop (₹999).
- Result: Crossed ₹1.2L/month income.

Lesson: He didn't quit his job. He **layered smartly**.

Section 6: Mentor's 3 Golden Rules

1. **Stabilize First, Then Add** – Don't juggle five streams when none are stable.
2. **Make Streams Complement Each Other** – e.g., service → product → affiliate.
3. **Never Depend Fully on One Platform** – Clients, Instagram, YouTube—anything can vanish.

Section 7: Framework – The 3 Levels of Hustle Income

- **Level 1: Active Hustle Income**
- Freelancing, part-time business, service work.
- **Level 2: Semi-Passive Income**
- Digital products, affiliates, small courses.
- **Level 3: Wealth Streams**
- Investments, royalties, equity.

Move step by step. Don't chase Level 3 before you nail Level 1 & 2.

Section 8: Mentor Story – How I Learned the Hard Way

In my first year, I put all energy into client projects. It was good money, but exhausting. When one client ghosted me, my income halved overnight.

That's when I created my first **mini digital product**—a funnel template. It made just ₹5,000 the first month, but I'll never forget that feeling. That little stream gave me confidence: "I'm not fully dependent anymore."

From there, I stacked: client work → products → coaching → affiliates.
And that's exactly how I scaled into financial freedom.

Section 9: Worksheets

Worksheet 1 – Map Your Current Streams

Stream Active / Passive Income Today Target in 6 Months

Job / Freelance. Active. ₹_____ ₹_____

Product / Course Semi-Passive ₹_____ ₹_____

Investments. Passive ₹_____ ₹_____

Worksheet 2 – Your "Next Stream" Plan

Answer these questions:

1. What is my current main income stream?
2. How can I turn part of it into a product or system?
3. What's one related stream I can add in the next 3 months?

Section 10: Reflection Exercise

Write down:

- If your **main income stopped tomorrow**, how many streams would still keep you afloat?
- What **one new stream** can you realistically start in the next 90 days?

Section 11: Warning – The Shiny Object Syndrome

Most people fail not because they lack streams, but because they chase too many. Crypto today, dropshipping tomorrow, then quitting everything.

Rule: *More streams doesn't mean more chaos—it means smarter stacking.*

Section 12: Mentor's Note – The Power of Options

When you have one stream, you live in fear: "What if it goes away?"

When you have three streams, you live in freedom: "Even if one fails, I'm safe."

That's the power of multiple streams. Not just money. **Options. Choices. Independence.**

1. Why You Need Multiple Streams (Story + Reality Check)

I'll share a quick story.

When I first started freelancing, I depended only on Fiverr. Business was great for a few months—until one day, Fiverr changed its algorithm and my gigs stopped ranking. My income fell to almost zero overnight.

That shock taught me a life-long lesson: never rely on a single platform, client, or hustle.

From there, I diversified:

- **Freelancing** for quick income.
- **Content creation** to build long-term authority.
- **Affiliate marketing** for passive income.
- **Digital products** like eBooks and templates.

That combination became unshakable. Even if one dipped, others kept me afloat.

Lesson: Even beginners can set up at least two streams: one **active hustle** (freelancing/service) and one **scalable hustle** (content, affiliate, or product).

2. Types of Hustle Income Streams

Here are five categories you can mix and match:

Freelancing Income (short-term, skill-based, quick money).

- Platforms: Fiverr, Upwork, PeoplePerHour.
- Examples: graphic design, copywriting, video editing.

Content Creation Income (authority + brand).

- Platforms: YouTube, Instagram, LinkedIn, Medium.
- Monetization: ads, sponsorships, affiliate links.

Affiliate Marketing Income (low-cost, scalable).

- Promote tools you use (Hostinger, Systeme.io, Canva, etc.).
- Earn commission per sale without creating products.

Digital Product Income (one-time work, infinite sales).

- E-books, templates, checklists, online courses.

Small Business/Service Income (local or online).

- Social media management for small businesses.
- Coaching or consulting.

3. The 2×2 Hustle Model

When starting, you don't need all five streams. That's overwhelming. Instead, pick:

- **1 Active Hustle** (brings immediate cash)
- **1 Scalable Hustle** (builds long-term growth)

Example:

- Freelancing + Affiliate Marketing
- Content Creation + Digital Products
- Service Business + Course Building

This balance gives you both **short-term survival money** and **long-term wealth potential.**

4. Case Studies of Hustlers with Multiple Streams

Ravi (Freelancer + Affiliate)

- Started as a video editor on Fiverr. Added affiliate links to editing software he used. His freelancing paid the bills, his affiliate side started growing, and within a year he doubled his monthly income.

Priya (Content + Digital Product)

- She began posting Instagram reels about productivity. After 6 months, she launched a ₹299 Notion template pack. Her audience snapped it up—her first ₹50k came in one week.

Amit (Service + Coaching)

- He helped local shopkeepers run Facebook ads. Later, he packaged his knowledge into a coaching program for aspiring freelancers. That gave him stability and higher margins.

5. Exercise: Designing Your Income Streams

👉 **Step 1:** Write down your current main hustle (freelancing, job, content, etc.).

👉 **Step 2:** Choose 1 additional scalable hustle (affiliate, product, or content).

👉 **Step 3:** Write a 3-month plan to start both in parallel.

Worksheet Prompt (Fill-in-the-Blank):

- My active hustle is: ____________
- My scalable hustle is: ____________
- In the next 90 days, I will:

1.
2.
3.

BONUS: Hustle Blueprints

To make this chapter 100% actionable, here are 3 **ready-to-use side hustle blueprints** you can copy-paste into your life:

1. Freelance + Course Path

- Month 1–2: Start freelancing on Fiverr/Upwork in your skill.
- Month 3: Document your process as a mini-course (₹499–₹999).
- Month 6: Launch your course to the same audience.

✅ Outcome: Cash flow from freelancing + scalable income from course.

2. Content + Affiliate Path

- Month 1: Pick a platform (YouTube/Instagram/LinkedIn). Start posting 3×/week.
- Month 2–3: Add affiliate links to the tools you use in your niche.
- Month 6: Start earning affiliate sales while growing your authority.

✅ Outcome: Content builds brand, affiliate builds passive income.

3. Service + Product Path

- Month 1: Offer a service (social media management, ads, funnels).
- Month 2: Build templates/checklists from your service process.
- Month 4: Sell those templates as a low-ticket digital product.

✅ Outcome: Active income + semi-passive income.

Takeaway:

Your first goal is **2 streams, not 7.** Keep it simple, but always think: *"How can I turn this into another stream without doubling my workload?"*

30

Building Your Personal Brand

So far, you've learned how to start, earn, and build multiple streams of income. But here's the truth: **without a personal brand, you'll always remain replaceable.**

A logo can be copied. A service can be copied. Even your prices can be beaten.

But your **brand—your voice, your story, your trust—is uncopyable.**

This chapter will show you how to build that brand, step by step, even if you're starting from zero.

1. What is a Personal Brand (and Why It Matters)?

Your personal brand is simply **how people remember you** when you're not in the room.

- Do they see you as an expert?
- Do they feel you're trustworthy?
- Do they think, *"Oh, this is the person who helps with X problem"*?

When your brand is strong, you stop begging for clients—opportunities come looking for you.

Real Talk:

When I began freelancing, I was just another profile on Fiverr. But when I started sharing my story and tips on LinkedIn, people saw me as more than a seller—they saw me as a **guide.** That shift brought in better-paying clients *outside the platform.*

2. The 3 Pillars of a Strong Personal Brand

Clarity – Be clear on what you stand for.

- Example: "I help small businesses grow with simple ads."
- Exercise: Write your **one-line identity statement**:
- *"I help [who] achieve [what] using [how]."*

Consistency – People should see you regularly.

- Posting once in 3 months won't build trust.
- Even 2–3 posts per week make a big difference.

Credibility – Show proof, not just promises.

- Share results, testimonials, case studies, or even your own journey.
- Example: "Here's how I made my first ₹10k freelancing—step by step."

3. Where to Build Your Brand (Platforms that Matter)

Not all platforms are equal. Pick **one main stage** and **one support stage.**

- **LinkedIn** → Best for freelancers, consultants, service hustles.
- **Instagram** → Best for creators, lifestyle niches, visual products.

- **YouTube** → Best for building authority, evergreen growth.
- **Twitter/X** → Best for fast, niche insights, networking.

Pro Tip: Start where your potential clients hang out—not where your friends hang out.

4. Storytelling: The Secret Weapon

People don't connect with data; they connect with **stories.**
Every small win in your side hustle can be turned into a story:

- "I got my first client with zero experience."
- "I worked 1 hour/day and made my first ₹10k."
- "Here's what I learned failing my first YouTube channel."

Stories make you **relatable**. And relatability = trust.

5. Exercise: Your Brand Starter Pack

Fill this out to design your **personal brand foundation:**

- My 1-line identity statement: ___________________________
- My primary platform: ___________________________
- My posting frequency (realistic): ___________________________
- My first 3 story ideas:

1.
2.
3.

6. Case Studies – Beginner Brands That Worked

- **Nisha (Freelance Writer)**
- Started posting short LinkedIn posts about "mistakes small businesses make in blogs." Within 3 months, she had inbound clients paying double her Upwork rates.
- **Rohit (Fitness Hustle)**
- Began posting Instagram reels of 10-min workouts he did at home. After 6 months, he launched a ₹499 workout challenge. His audience trusted him because they saw his face daily.
- **Sanya (Tech Tutor)**
- Posted YouTube videos teaching Excel tips. Grew slowly but steadily. By the 1-year mark, she was earning ad revenue + selling her Excel templates on Gumroad.

7. Reflection: Are You a Hidden Expert?

Here's a truth bomb: most beginners already have skills, but no one knows about them.

Your personal brand is just making your skills **visible to the right people.**

So ask yourself:

"What do I want to be known for 6 months from now?"

"If people Googled me, what should they find?"

Key Takeaway

Your personal brand is your **long-term insurance policy.** Hustles may change, platforms may change, but once people trust YOU, they'll follow you anywhere.

Worksheet Prompt

1. Write your **Identity Statement.**
2. Pick **one platform** to commit to.
3. Draft your **first 3 posts/stories.**
4. Share your story publicly this week.

Networking & Collaboration

When I started my first hustle, I believed the myth: *"If I work hard alone, I'll win big."*

But here's the truth I learned the hard way: **your network is your shortcut.**

Opportunities don't just appear out of thin air. They come from people.

Clients, mentors, partners, collaborators—these are the bridges that turn a ₹10k hustle into a ₹1 lakh+ business.

1. Why Networking Isn't "Sleazy"

For many middle-class beginners, networking feels like "using" people. But think about it differently:

Networking = **value exchange.**

You give value, you get value.

You help someone, they help you back.

It's not about faking friendships—it's about building **real relationships** with people who are also hustling.

Personal Note:

The biggest shift in my journey came when I stopped trying to be a lone wolf. I joined online communities, messaged peers, and shared small tips for free. Within weeks, opportunities I could never have found alone started opening up.

2. The 3 Circles of Networking

Peers – People on the same journey as you.

- Example: Other freelancers, YouTubers, side hustlers.
- Why: They motivate you, share struggles, and sometimes share clients.

Mentors – People 5–10 steps ahead.

- Why: They cut your learning curve in half.
- Pro Tip: Don't ask, "Can you mentor me?" Instead, add value—share their work, comment thoughtfully, apply their lessons.

Collaborators – People you can partner with.

- Example: A writer teams up with a designer → offers "content + design" package.
- Example: A fitness coach teams up with a dietitian → offers "workout + diet" challenge.

3. Platforms to Find Your Tribe

- **LinkedIn** → Comment on posts in your niche, message peers.
- **Facebook/WhatsApp Groups** → Still powerful for freelancers and hobby-based hustles.
- **Discord/Slack Communities** → Great for tech, gaming, or creative hustles.
- **Offline Events** → Even local meetups or co-working hubs can give big breakthroughs.

Don't try to be everywhere. Pick 1–2 platforms and show up consistently.

4. Collaboration in Action: Mini Case Studies

Neha (Freelancer)

- Started writing blogs but struggled to find design clients. Partnered with a designer. Together they offered "Blog + Graphics" packages. Clients loved the one-stop solution → doubled income.

Ravi (YouTuber)

- Instead of competing, he did collaboration videos with other small YouTubers. Both audiences cross-pollinated. His subscriber growth doubled in 3 months.

Amit (Coach)

- Teaming up with a finance YouTuber, he ran a free webinar → both gained hundreds of new email subscribers for their paid programs.

5. Simple First Steps to Network (Even if You're Shy)

1. **Comment daily** on 3–5 posts in your niche (LinkedIn, Insta, Twitter).
2. **Message one person per week**:

"Hey, loved your post on X. I tried your tip—it worked. Thanks for sharing!"

1. **Join one community**: online or offline.
2. **Offer collaboration**: "I do X, you do Y. Let's try something together."

6. Exercise – Your Networking Plan

Fill this out (and stick it on your wall):

- My **primary networking platform**: ________________________
- My **weekly action**: Comment on ___ posts, message ___ new people.
- My **collaboration idea**: ________________________

7. Key Takeaway

Your hustle may start alone, but it won't grow alone.
The right people will open doors that years of solo grinding never could.

Mini-Checklist: Networking & Collaboration

✅ Engage (don't just scroll).
✅ Add value before asking.
✅ Partner where it creates win-win offers.
✅ Stay consistent—relationships compound over time.

Networking & Collaboration (Expanded with Collaboration Matrix)

(continuation from the draft above...)

The Collaboration Matrix: Map Your Network

One of the most powerful exercises you can do right now is to create a **Collaboration Matrix**—a simple tool to see *who's already in your circle, who you should connect with, and how you can create win-win opportunities.*

Think of it as your personal "hustle relationship map."

How It Works

Draw a simple 3×3 grid (you can sketch it on paper, use Excel, or even Notion/Google Docs). The three categories are:

1. **Peers** → People on the same journey as you (freelancers, creators, side hustlers).
2. **Mentors** → People 5–10 steps ahead of you (thought leaders, coaches, successful entrepreneurs).

Collaborators → People with complementary skills/products you can partner with.

Step 1 – Fill It In

- Write down at least **3 names in each category** (peers, mentors, collaborators).
- If you can't think of names right now, write "To Find" and make it a goal to identify them within a week.

Step 2 – Value First

Networking flips when you **give before asking.**
Examples:

- Share someone's work on LinkedIn.
- Offer a testimonial if you used their advice.
- Refer a client or opportunity their way.

This makes you memorable and likable without "begging for help."

Step 3 – Action Steps

Write **one action per person** you want to connect with. Keep it small and specific (comment, DM, pitch a collab, attend a webinar).

Consistency beats intensity. Doing one meaningful networking action daily will compound into dozens of strong connections in 6 months.

Reflection Exercise – Your 90-Day Networking Goal

Answer these prompts in your journal:

1. **By the end of 90 days, I want to have connected with ___ new peers.**
2. **I will approach ___ mentors by engaging with their content.**
3. **I will test ___ collaborations (joint project, webinar, video, etc.).**

Key Takeaway (Expanded)

Your hustle won't grow in isolation.

Your **Collaboration Matrix** is your map to scale faster, smarter, and with less stress.

- Peers keep you motivated.
- Mentors shorten your learning curve.
- Collaborators multiply your reach and revenue.

When you put this matrix into practice, you stop hustling alone and start hustling as part of a **network-driven growth machine.**

Mini-Checklist: Collaboration in Action (Expanded)

✅ Fill out your Collaboration Matrix with at least 9 names.
✅ Add value first before asking for help.
✅ Take 1 small action per person per week.
✅ Review your matrix monthly and update it.

31

Building Your Personal Brand

"Your brand is what people say about you when you're not in the room."
– Jeff Bezos

Have you ever wondered why some freelancers, creators, or side hustlers seem to attract opportunities effortlessly, while others struggle to get noticed? The difference isn't always skill—it's **brand presence**. Your personal brand is the **magnet that draws clients, collaborations, and opportunities** to you.

When I started scaling my side hustles, I realized that delivering value wasn't enough. People needed to **recognize my expertise, trust me, and remember me**. That's when I focused on building my personal brand. Overnight, networking became easier, clients reached out without me pitching aggressively, and my income streams began to multiply.

Why Personal Branding Matters

1. **Visibility:** People can't hire or follow you if they don't know you exist.
2. **Trust:** A strong personal brand signals credibility and authority.
3. **Leverage:** Opportunities flow in without constant outreach.

4. **Scalability:** Your brand amplifies all your income streams.

I once worked silently on a freelance project for months. When I started sharing my process, tips, and results on social media, inquiries flooded in. Just by **showing my journey**, I became more visible than competitors with the same skill set. This taught me that **brand perception often matters more than raw talent**.

Step 1: Define Your Brand Identity

Your brand is not just a logo or a website—it's a **clear message about who you are, what you offer, and why people should care**.

Ask yourself:

- What is my unique skill or expertise?
- Who is my target audience?
- What problem do I solve for them?
- What values do I want to communicate?

Exercise:

Write a **2–3 sentence brand statement** answering the above questions. This is your personal brand elevator pitch.

Step 2: Show Up Consistently

Consistency is the heartbeat of branding. You don't need fancy designs or viral content—just **regular, value-driven presence**.

- Share your journey, tips, and lessons learned.
- Post 2–3 times per week on a chosen platform (LinkedIn, Instagram, YouTube, or blog).
- Engage with your audience through comments, DMs, and collaborations.

I started posting short tutorials and insights on Instagram every week. Within 3 months, I gained a small but highly engaged following. Those followers turned into clients, course students, and collaborators. **Consistency created credibility** and multiplied opportunities.

Exercise:

Create a 7-**day content plan**: what you will post each day, including tips, lessons, or personal stories.

Step 3: Leverage Multiple Channels

You don't have to be everywhere, but using **multiple channels strategically** expands reach:

- **Social Media:** Share insights, behind-the-scenes, client success stories.
- **Blog or Medium:** Long-form content builds authority and helps with discovery.
- **Email Newsletter:** Build a direct line to your audience and sell services/products.
- **YouTube / Podcasts:** Showcase expertise, personality, and stories.

Exercise:

Select **2 platforms to start with**, and create your **first piece of branded content** for each.

Step 4: Authentic Storytelling

People connect with **stories, not sales pitches**. Share your journey, failures, small wins, and lessons learned. This makes your brand human and relatable.

I once shared my first failed freelance attempt—losing ₹5,000 due to inexperience. That post got more engagement than any technical tip I had shared. People related to my struggle, trusted my guidance, and later became clients.

Exercise:
Write a **short story (200–300 words)** about a challenge you overcame in your side hustle or career. Share it online this week.

Step 5: Build Authority Through Value

A strong personal brand isn't about bragging—it's about **helping others achieve results**.

- Share tips, hacks, and tutorials.
- Highlight results you helped clients or peers achieve.
- Use testimonials and case studies to reinforce credibility.

Exercise:
List **3 ways you can provide tangible value** to your audience this month. Create one piece of content for each.

Step 6: Monetize Your Brand

Once you've established visibility and trust, your personal brand can **amplify your income streams**:

- Freelance clients will find you.
- Courses, workshops, or coaching can sell faster.
- Affiliate or product promotions become more effective.

Case Study:
Rahul, a beginner content creator I mentored, started with YouTube tutorials. Within 6 months, his small following became a **paid course audience**, and he monetized affiliate tools. His personal brand **turned his**

side hustle into his main income source.

Exercise:
Identify **one monetization path** tied to your brand this month (course, service, affiliate, etc.) and draft a **launch plan with 3 actionable steps**.

Key Takeaways

- Your personal brand is your **magnet for opportunities**.
- Define your identity, be consistent, and share your authentic story.
- Use 2–3 strategic channels to amplify reach.
- Provide value first; monetize second.
- A strong brand multiplies all your side hustle income streams.

Remember: People don't just buy services—they buy **trust, results, and the story behind the person delivering them**. Your brand is that story.

Next Exercise:

1. Write your **brand statement** in 2–3 sentences.
2. Plan your **first** 7 **days of content** and post it.
3. Choose **2 platforms** to start building presence.
4. Share your **authentic story** online.
5. Identify **one monetization path** tied to your brand and draft actionable steps.

32

Building Your Personal Brand

"Your brand is what people say about you when you're not in the room." – Jeff Bezos

Have you ever wondered why some side hustlers effortlessly attract clients, followers, and opportunities while others struggle despite working just as hard? Could the difference be **how they are perceived** in their industry?

When I started freelancing, I delivered quality work, but I struggled to get repeat clients. It wasn't about skill—it was about **visibility, trust, and positioning**. Once I focused on building my personal brand, things changed: clients reached out, collaborations appeared, and my hustles started scaling faster than I had imagined.

Why Personal Branding Matters

1. **Trust & Credibility:** People buy from those they know, like, and trust.
2. **Attracting Clients & Opportunities:** A strong brand brings inbound inquiries.
3. **Higher Value & Pricing Power:** Branding allows you to charge more

confidently.

4. **Foundation for Multiple Hustles:** One strong brand can support freelancing, products, and content simultaneously.

I remember posting my first series of tutorials online. At first, barely anyone noticed. But after consistently sharing insights and client successes, I started receiving messages like: *"I want to work with you"* and *"Can you guide me on starting my own hustle?"* My personal brand became a **magnet for opportunities**.

Step 1: Define Your Brand Identity

Ask yourself:

- What am I passionate about?
- What problems do I solve?
- Who is my ideal audience?

Your brand identity is **not just a logo or color palette**—it's **your story, expertise, and personality expressed consistently**.

Exercise:

Write a **50-word personal brand statement** that answers: "I help [audience] achieve [result] by [your method]." Example: *"I help freelancers build their first ₹10k/month side hustle by teaching them simple, actionable strategies they can implement today."*

Step 2: Position Yourself as an Expert

- Share results, case studies, and learnings from your hustles.
- Write blogs, create videos, or post social media updates.
- Be generous with value, not just promotion.

When I began sharing client success stories and small wins from my hustles, I started receiving **referrals organically**. People trusted my methods because I demonstrated results.

Exercise:

Post **one valuable tip or case study this week** on your preferred platform. Track engagement and learn what resonates.

Step 3: Build Consistent Visibility

- Post regularly to stay top-of-mind.
- Engage with your audience: answer questions, comment, and share insights.
- Maintain consistency in your messaging and visual identity.

Mini-Blueprint:

- Platform focus: LinkedIn, Instagram, or YouTube (choose 1–2)
- Posting cadence: 2–3 posts per week
- Engagement: reply to every comment or message within 24 hours

Exercise:

Create a **1-week content plan**: 3 posts, 2 stories, 1 live session or video. Stick to it.

Step 4: Leverage Testimonials & Social Proof

- Showcase client success stories.
- Highlight milestones: revenue growth, completed projects, or collaborations.
- Encourage reviews and recommendations.

I once featured a freelancer I mentored who hit their first ₹50k month.

Sharing this success not only inspired others but also **built my credibility as a trusted guide**, leading to more high-value clients.

Exercise:
Ask **3 satisfied clients or collaborators** for a testimonial this week. Use it in your online profiles or portfolio.

Step 5: Extend Your Brand Across Multiple Hustles

Your personal brand should **support all your side hustles**:

- Freelancing → showcase your expertise
- Digital products → demonstrate authority
- Content → engage and educate your audience

Exercise:
List **all your current and potential hustles**. Write 1–2 sentences for each, explaining **how your brand positions you as the go-to person**.

Key Takeaways

- A strong personal brand **builds trust, attracts clients, and accelerates growth**.
- Position yourself consistently, share results, and engage with your audience.
- Testimonials and social proof multiply credibility.
- One personal brand can amplify multiple side hustles simultaneously.

Remember: People don't just buy products or services—they **buy confidence, trust, and expertise**. Your brand is the bridge that turns your side hustles into sustainable financial freedom.

Next Exercises:

1. Draft your **50-word personal brand statement**.
2. Share **one valuable tip or case study** this week online.
3. Build a **1-week content plan** for posting and engagement.
4. Collect **3 testimonials** from clients or collaborators.
5. Map **how your brand supports all your hustles** in 1–2 sentences each.

33

Building Multiple Streams of Income

"*Never put all your eggs in one basket.*"

If there's one principle that separates long-term wealth builders from casual hustlers, it's **income diversification**. The middle-class trap often comes from relying on **one paycheck**, and even many side hustlers fall into the same trap if they focus on a single hustle.

1. Why Multiple Income Streams Matter

Relying on one income source is risky:

- Illness, layoffs, or market changes can wipe out a single income source.
- Your earning potential is capped by time and energy.

The solution:
Create **at least 3 income streams** that feed into your finances:

1. **Active Income** – your main hustle or job.
2. **Semi-Passive Income** – small digital products, courses, affiliate commissions.
3. **Passive Income** – investments, royalties, or subscription models.

Personal Note:

When I first started, I had a freelance writing hustle (active), sold a mini course (semi-passive), and then added affiliate promotions (passive). Within 12 months, these three streams collectively outperformed my 9-to-5 salary.

2. Case Study 1 – Freelance to Multi-Stream Hustler

Ravi's Story:

Ravi was a college graduate stuck in a 9-to-5 job. He started freelancing as a graphic designer:

- Month 1: ₹5,000 from one client.
- Month 3: Added 2 clients → ₹15,000.
- Month 6: Created a mini Canva course → ₹10,000 revenue.
- Month 9: Started an affiliate partnership promoting design tools → ₹5,000/month passive income.

Lesson: Small wins in one stream can be reinvested to build new streams.

Exercise:

1. List your **current active income stream**.
2. Brainstorm **2 ways to create semi-passive income** related to it.
3. Identify **1 potential passive stream** to start exploring this month.

3. Case Study 2 – Content Creator Path

Anita's Story:

Anita started a YouTube channel teaching easy recipes:

- Month 1–2: Built an audience → monetized through ads → ₹2,000/month.
- Month 3: Created a digital recipe eBook → ₹8,000 revenue.
- Month 4–6: Offered virtual cooking workshops → ₹15,000.

- Month 6: Partnered with a kitchenware brand for affiliate commissions → ₹5,000/month.

Key Takeaway: Content + product + affiliate = multiple income streams, all leveraging the same initial hustle.

Exercise:

- Map your **current audience or skill**.
- Identify **3 monetization opportunities** you can pursue simultaneously.

4. The Multi-Stream Blueprint

Here's a **simple framework** to help readers structure income streams without overwhelm:

Stream Type Examples Time Commitment Initial Investment Goal in 3 Months

Active Income. Freelance, 9-to-5, coaching High. Low. ₹5k–₹10k

Semi-Passive Online course, eBook, service package, Medium, Medium. ₹5k–₹15k

Passive Income. Affiliate, subscription, royalties, Low. Low–Medium. ₹2k–₹10k

Exercise:

- Fill out this table for your hustles.
- Set **specific income targets** for each stream in the next 3 months.

5. Tips to Avoid Overwhelm

1. **Start small:** Don't try 5 streams at once; start with one active + one semi-passive.
2. **Leverage existing skills:** Build new streams from what you already know.
3. **Automate early:** Use scheduling, email sequences, or templates.
4. **Track results:** Know which streams perform best → double down there.

Personal Note:

When I added an affiliate stream to my writing hustle, I spent just 1 hour setting up a funnel. Within 30 days, it made ₹4,000/month—without touching my main hustle. That's the magic of multi-stream thinking.

6. Reflection Exercise – Your Income Streams Roadmap

Answer these:

1. Which income stream gives you **immediate cash flow**?
2. Which stream can **scale semi-passively** in the next 60 days?
3. What **passive income opportunity** can I start exploring this month with minimal risk?

Draw a simple map of **all 3 streams**, showing **current → short-term → long-term goals**.

7. Mini-Checklist – Building Multiple Streams

✅ Identify at least **3 streams** of income.
✅ Start with one active + one semi-passive this month.
✅ Reinvest first earnings from each stream into another.
✅ Track performance weekly; double down on the highest ROI streams.

✅ Set **3-month income targets** for each stream.

8. Bonus: Sample Hustle Blueprints

Here are three **ready-to-use paths** to get readers thinking strategically:

Freelance + Course Path

- Active: Freelance writing/design
- Semi-passive: Mini online course teaching the skill
- Passive: Affiliate tools/resources for students

Content + Affiliate Path

- Active: YouTube/Blog
- Semi-passive: eBook or template sales
- Passive: Affiliate commissions on recommended products

Service + Digital Product Path

- Active: Coaching, consulting, or local service
- Semi-passive: Paid worksheets, guides, templates
- Passive: Subscription membership or mastermind

Tip: Pick one blueprint that resonates, tweak to your skillset, and take action immediately.

Key Takeaways (Expanded)

- Diversification reduces risk, increases growth, and builds wealth faster.
- Start small: one active + one semi-passive + explore passive income.
- Reinvest earnings to accelerate growth.

- Use case studies and blueprints as inspiration—don't copy blindly.

34

From Hustler to Entrepreneur

When I first started, I thought a side hustle was "extra cash in my pocket."

But here's what I learned: **side hustles are just the training wheels.**

If you want to escape the middle-class trap and build lasting wealth, you must shift your thinking from **"I'm earning extra" → "I'm building a business."**

1. The Hustler vs. Entrepreneur Mindset

Aspect Hustler Mindset Entrepreneur Mindset

Focus Short-term income Long-term growth & systems

Decision-making Reactive Strategic & proactive

Goal Make more money Build sustainable, recurring revenue

Risk approach. Avoid big risks. Take calculated risks+planning

Personal Note:

When I treated my first ₹10k/month side hustle like a business, I started planning for the next ₹50k → ₹1 lakh, instead of just celebrating the "extra cash." This shift alone multiplied my income faster than any new hustle idea could.

2. Systematizing Your Hustle

To grow, you need **systems**:

1. **Operations** → How you deliver value consistently.
2. **Marketing** → How you get clients/customers automatically.
3. **Finance** → Track income, reinvest profits, manage cash flow.

Even simple systems (Google Sheets, Notion, automated emails) make a side hustle feel like a business.

Exercise – Your First System Blueprint:

- Write down 3 repeatable tasks you do every week for your side hustle.
- How can you automate or systematize them in the next 30 days?

3. Scaling Small Wins Into Revenue Streams

- Side Hustle → Main Income: Pick your most profitable hustle and double down.
- Main Income → Multiple Streams: Add complementary products/services (ex: freelancing + course + affiliate).
- Example: I started with content writing → added a small digital course → started consulting → now my side hustles feed into each other.

Exercise – Multi-Stream Plan:

1. List your top-performing hustle.
2. Brainstorm 2 complementary streams you can add.

3. Pick one to start next month.

4. Teaming Up to Grow Faster

Once you have processes, consider **outsourcing or collaborating**:

- Virtual assistants for repetitive tasks.
- Designers or editors for content.
- Strategic partners to co-launch products.

Mini-case study:

A friend of mine outsourced design and email automation after earning ₹20k/month. Within 3 months, he freed 20 hours/week and doubled revenue without working extra hours.

5. Mindset Shifts for Entrepreneurs

1. Stop thinking in "hours → money." Think in **value → income**.
2. Treat every client/customer as a **mini-business opportunity**.
3. Invest in **learning systems, marketing, and collaboration skills**.

Exercise – Entrepreneur Mindset Reflection:

- What's one mindset habit I need to adopt this week to treat my hustle like a business?
- What repetitive task can I systematize or outsource this month?

6. Key Takeaway

Your side hustle is the **seed**. Treat it like a business, systematize it, and scale small wins into multiple income streams. This is the bridge from **extra cash → financial independence**.

Mini-Checklist: From Hustler to Entrepreneur

✅ Identify your most profitable hustle.
  ✅ Create simple systems for operations, marketing, and finance.
  ✅ Brainstorm at least 2 complementary revenue streams.
  ✅ Test one collaboration or outsourcing opportunity this month.

35

Networking & Collaboration

"Your network determines your net worth."

By now, you've built side hustles, small wins, multiple income streams, and a personal brand. But to scale faster, you need to **connect with the right people**, collaborate strategically, and leverage relationships to open doors that would take years to reach alone.

1. Why Networking & Collaboration Matter

Many side hustlers and freelancers stay trapped in isolation. They work hard, but opportunities are limited by **who they know**.

Smart networking and collaborations allow you to:

- Gain **new clients or customers** without cold outreach.
- Learn from **mentors and peers** who've done it before.
- Access **partnership opportunities** that multiply revenue.
- Expand your **personal brand reach** naturally.

Personal Note:

I learned early on that showing up alone can get you only so far. Once I started connecting with peers and mentors online, opportunities started flowing—joint workshops, referrals, and collaborative projects that brought in revenue I hadn't imagined in my first year.

2. Case Study 1 – The Freelance Collaboration Boost

Ravi's Story:

Ravi was a freelance graphic designer struggling to land consistent clients. He started reaching out to other freelancers and small digital agencies to **offer joint projects**.

Actions:

1. Collaborated on **website design + copywriting packages** with a freelance writer.
2. Partnered with a social media manager to offer **complete brand packages**.
3. Engaged in **online communities**, offering free tips and advice.

Results:

- Revenue jumped from ₹10k/month → ₹50k/month within 4 months.
- Gained **referrals through collaborators' networks**.
- Built long-term partnerships that generated repeat business.

Lesson: Collaboration multiplies reach and income faster than solo work.

Exercise:

- List **5 potential collaborators** in your niche.
- Note **how each collaboration could benefit both sides**.

3. Case Study 2 – Strategic Networking Online

Priya's Story:

Priya was an aspiring content creator with a small Instagram following. She wanted to grow her online presence.

Actions:

1. Joined **relevant Facebook & LinkedIn groups**.
2. Commented on industry leaders' posts with **insightful feedback**.
3. Sent **personalized connection messages** to 10 mentors weekly.

Results:

- Gained **1000+ targeted followers** in 2 months.
- Invited to **collaborative podcasts & webinars** → revenue + brand credibility.
- Built relationships that turned into **paid mentorships and collaborations**.

Lesson: Networking isn't just about quantity—it's **quality** + **consistent engagement**.

4. Building Your Collaboration Matrix

A **Collaboration Matrix** helps you visualize **who to connect with, why, and how to act**.

Step 1 – Identify Categories:

- Peers: People doing similar side hustles or businesses.
- Mentors: Experienced professionals in your niche.
- Collaborators: Complementary skill sets (designer + copywriter, freelancer + course creator).
- Influencers: People with large audiences who can amplify your reach.

Step 2 – Rate Potential Value:

- Skills: How their expertise complements yours.
- Reach: How big or engaged is their audience.
- Mutual Benefit: What value you can offer them.

Step 3 – Action Plan:

- Reach out with a **personalized proposal** or value-driven collaboration idea.
- Set goals for **connection attempts weekly/monthly**.
- Track outcomes and adjust your approach.

5. Best Practices for Networking & Collaboration

1. **Give Before You Take** – Offer value first. Share tips, advice, or resources.
2. **Follow Up Consistently** – Relationships grow with attention and care.
3. **Be Genuine** – Don't network just for money; build authentic connections.
4. **Leverage Online & Offline** – Social media, communities, and meetups.
5. **Document Your Network** – Keep track of contacts, interactions, and opportunities.

Tip: Networking isn't a one-time event—it's **a habit, like daily posting or skill-building**.

6. Exercises – Build Your Network

1. **List 10 people** you admire or want to collaborate with.
2. Write a **personalized message** to 3 people this week.
3. Identify **3 online communities or events** to join this month.
4. Note **2 collaborations** that could bring immediate value.
5. Track **weekly progress**: new connections, messages sent, meetings scheduled.

7. Personal Story – My Collaboration Wins

I started small. One mentor suggested **guest posting on a newsletter**, another freelancer collaborated on a mini-course. Within 3 months:

- Side income doubled.
- My audience grew exponentially.
- More people started **inviting me to joint projects**.

Key takeaway: You can't do everything alone. Strategic collaboration **accelerates growth** and opens doors that hard work alone might take years to reach.

36

Scaling Your Hustle Into Sustainable Income Streams

"Don't just earn once; build a system that earns while you sleep."

By now, you've built your side hustle, achieved small wins, developed multiple streams, cultivated a personal brand, and expanded your network. The next step is **systematically scaling** these efforts into sustainable income streams that keep growing without burning you out.

1. Why Scaling Matters

Most side hustlers plateau because they **focus on trading hours for money**. Sustainable income comes when you:

- Convert time-bound tasks into systems or products.
- Multiply revenue without multiplying effort.
- Reinvest profits into higher-value opportunities.

Personal Note:

I remember my first ₹10k month as a freelancer—it felt amazing. But I quickly realized that to reach ₹1 lakh/month, I needed systems, collaborations, and scalable offerings rather than just working harder.

2. Case Study 1 – From Freelancer to Online Course Creator

Ankit's Story:

Ankit started as a freelance content writer, earning ₹15k/month. He wanted more freedom and higher income.

Steps he took:

1. Documented his **freelance process into a mini-guide**.
2. Created a **low-cost online course** teaching others his method.
3. Leveraged his **freelance network** for initial buyers.
4. Automated delivery via a simple **email funnel**.

Results:

- Monthly income increased from ₹15k → ₹50k within 2 months.
- Course sold continuously **without him working extra hours**.
- Free time increased, allowing focus on creating additional courses.

Lesson: Packaging your skills into products allows your side hustle to scale infinitely.

Exercise:

- List one **skill or process** you could turn into a product or course this month.
- Identify your **first 10 potential customers** and plan how to reach them.

3. Case Study 2 – Side Hustle Bundles & Subscription Models

Sneha's Story:

Sneha was running a small Etsy store selling handmade planners. Her revenue was inconsistent, and she wanted predictability.

Steps she took:

1. Offered **monthly subscription boxes** with planners, stickers, and digital templates.
2. Promoted through her **Instagram and email list**.
3. Added **bonus workshops** for subscribers → increased perceived value.

Results:

- Revenue became **predictable each month**.
- Subscriber growth created **word-of-mouth referrals**.
- Could reinvest profits to create new products without affecting cash flow.

Lesson: Recurring income streams stabilize finances and allow you to plan growth strategically.

4. The Scaling Ladder

Think of scaling like climbing a ladder:

Step 1 – Optimize Current Hustle:

- Identify the **highest-earning activity**.
- Reduce tasks that don't generate revenue.

Step 2 – Package Your Expertise:

- Courses, templates, e-books, coaching sessions.
- Convert time-bound work into **repeatable products**.

Step 3 – Add Recurring Streams:

- Subscriptions, memberships, retainers.
- Aim for predictable monthly revenue.

Step 4 – Automate & Delegate:

- Use assistants, freelancers, or automation tools.
- Free up your time while the business continues growing.

Step 5 – Multiply via Partnerships:

- Collaborate with peers or influencers.
- Tap into **new audiences and revenue channels**.

Exercise:

- Draw your **own Scaling Ladder** with 3–5 steps for your side hustle.
- Write down **one action per step** to start implementing this week.

5. Mini Checklist – Scaling Essentials

Before you scale, ensure you've:

- Validated your side hustle idea with paying customers.
- Documented processes for repeatability.
- Identified at least **one scalable product or service**.
- Set up **systems for recurring revenue**.
- Built a **network and personal brand** to leverage collaborations.

Tip: Focus on **quality over quantity**. One scalable product executed well is better than ten half-baked ideas.

6. Reinvestment Strategy

Scaling requires reinvestment:

- **Profit → Marketing:** Boost visibility and attract more customers.
- **Profit → Tools/Automation:** Save time and increase efficiency.
- **Profit → Skills:** Learn advanced marketing, product creation, or leadership.

Personal Note:

I reinvested my first ₹50k into automation tools and small ad campaigns, which doubled my revenue in just two months. Reinvestment accelerates scaling far faster than relying solely on hard work.

Exercise:

- Allocate **30% of your next month's earnings** to scaling activities.
- List **3 areas where reinvestment will bring maximum impact**.

7. Reflection – Mindset for Sustainable Growth

Scaling is not just about money; it's about **long-term thinking, patience, and systems**. Ask yourself:

- Am I focusing on **short-term wins or long-term growth**?
- Which parts of my hustle can be **delegated or automated**?
- How can I **leverage relationships** for mutual growth?

Exercise:

- Write a **one-page vision** of where you want your side hustle to be in 6 months and 1 year.
- Highlight **3 actions** that will bring you closer to this vision.

Summary

Scaling your side hustle into sustainable income streams involves:

- Transforming skills into **repeatable, sellable products**.
- Adding **recurring revenue models** like subscriptions or memberships.
- Automating processes and delegating tasks.
- Reinvesting profits strategically.
- Leveraging collaborations, partnerships, and your personal brand.

By following these steps, your side hustle **transforms from a small experiment into a predictable, growing income machine**, giving you freedom and confidence to pursue larger financial goals.

37

Mastering Multiple Side Hustles

"Don't put all your eggs in one basket—but learn to manage the baskets effectively."

By now, you've built a side hustle, scaled it, and even created recurring revenue streams. But the real breakthrough for financial security comes when you **master multiple income streams**. This chapter will show you **how to manage, scale, and multiply side hustles without burning out**, giving you true freedom from the middle-class trap.

1. Why Multiple Side Hustles Matter

Relying on a single income source, even a successful one, keeps you **vulnerable to market changes, client churn, or personal emergencies**. Multiple side hustles:

- **Diversify risk** – if one income dips, others stabilize your cash flow.
- **Accelerate growth** – you can reinvest profits from one hustle into another.
- **Increase opportunities** – more chances to discover what really works.

Personal Note:

I started with one freelance skill. Within months, I added a small digital product, then a consulting service. By Month 6, I had three income streams, each contributing consistently to my monthly revenue. This strategy allowed me to experiment, learn fast, and scale without worrying about a single source drying up.

2. Case Study 1 – The Freelancer Who Became a Multi-Stream Entrepreneur

Rahul's Story:

Rahul was a web designer earning ₹20k/month. He wanted faster growth and more financial security.

Steps he took:

1. Continued his **freelance web projects** (primary income).
2. Created **pre-designed templates** and sold them on marketplaces (passive income).
3. Started **online workshops** teaching basic web design to students (semi-active income).

Results:

- Month 1: ₹20k → Month 3: ₹45k → Month 6: ₹80k.
- Income became **diverse and predictable**.
- He could **scale one stream while another ran on autopilot**.

Exercise:

- List **3 potential side hustles** you could manage simultaneously.
- Identify which one will be your **primary income generator** and which can be **passive/semi-passive**.

3. How to Choose Complementary Hustles

Not all hustles mix well. Pick ones that:

1. **Leverage your skills** – similar skill sets reduce the learning curve.
2. **Complement your audience** – one hustle can feed traffic or customers to another.
3. **Vary in time intensity** – mix active and passive streams.

Example:

- Freelancing + digital courses → Freelance work builds credibility; courses sell to the same audience.
- Content creation + affiliate marketing → You create content once, monetize multiple ways.

Exercise:

- Map your **current skill set vs. potential hustles**.
- Pick 2–3 complementary hustles that align with your goals.

4. Time Management for Multiple Hustles

Balancing multiple streams requires **planning, prioritization, and discipline**.

Mini-Checklist:

- Assign **time blocks** for each hustle.
- Focus on **high-value tasks first** (tasks that directly generate income).
- Automate or outsource **repetitive tasks**.
- Review progress **weekly** and adjust schedules.

Tip:

I personally use **1-hour focused sprints** per hustle daily. This keeps all streams moving without overwhelming my schedule.

5. Scaling Each Hustle Strategically

Scaling multiple hustles requires **different strategies for each income stream**:

1. **Primary Hustle:** Optimize, raise prices, add high-ticket clients.
2. **Secondary Hustle:** Automate and systematize for passive revenue.
3. **Tertiary Hustle:** Test new ideas, gather feedback, and iterate fast.

Case Study 2 – Sneha's Expansion:
Sneha had a small Etsy store (primary), a subscription box (secondary), and started affiliate content (tertiary).

- Primary: Optimize products and marketing → +30% revenue.
- Secondary: Outsource packaging → saved 10 hours/week.
- Tertiary: Published tutorials → generated small but growing passive income.

Lesson: Treat each hustle differently depending on its stage and revenue potential.

6. Reinvestment Across Hustles

Reinvest profits wisely:

- **Primary Hustle:** Reinvest in tools, marketing, or hiring help.
- **Secondary Hustle:** Scale automation and create additional products.
- **Tertiary Hustle:** Experiment with low-cost tests to find the next big opportunity.

Exercise:

- Allocate your **monthly profit** to each hustle based on growth potential.
- Write down **1 scaling action** for each hustle this month.

7. Mindset for Multi-Hustle Growth

- Accept that **not every hustle will succeed**. Failures teach lessons.
- Focus on **system-building rather than perfection**.
- Celebrate **small wins across all streams**, they compound into bigger success.

Personal Note:

When I managed multiple income streams, I initially felt stretched. But once I automated repetitive tasks and delegated, I realized **I was earning more by doing less**, and the multiple streams provided stability and confidence.

Reflection Exercise:

- Write down **3 fears or doubts** about managing multiple hustles.
- Write **3 strategies to overcome each fear**.

Summary

Mastering multiple side hustles involves:

- Choosing **complementary streams**.
- Strategically allocating **time, effort, and resources**.
- Scaling each hustle according to its **potential and maturity**.
- Reinvesting profits to grow and diversify income.
- Maintaining the **right mindset**, embracing failures, and celebrating progress.

By mastering this, you move from **earning one paycheck at a time** to **creating multiple, predictable income streams**, giving you the financial freedom to truly break free from the middle-class trap.

38

Your Personal 6-Month Multi-Hustle Action Plan

"Action is the bridge between dreams and results."

You've learned the mindset, built one or multiple side hustles, scaled your income, and even created complementary revenue streams. Now it's time to **turn theory into action**. This chapter lays out a **step-by-step, 6-month plan** that will help you implement everything you've learned so far and move toward **financial freedom and multi-stream income**.

1. The 6-Month Framework

To make real progress, we break down your journey into **6 monthly milestones**. Each month focuses on **specific actions** that are achievable, measurable, and build momentum.

Month 1 – Foundation:

- Identify **your primary and secondary side hustles**.
- Set up **tools, accounts, and workflow** for both.
- Exercise: Create a **1-week schedule** dedicating 1–2 hours/day per

hustle.

Month 2 – First Wins:

- Focus on **earning your first ₹5k–₹10k** from each hustle.
- Track progress daily and **reflect weekly**.
- Exercise: Write down **3 small wins** and **3 lessons** from the first month.

Month 3 – Streamlining & Automation:

- Identify **repetitive tasks** and automate where possible (emails, templates, social posting).
- Outsource or delegate small tasks if affordable.
- Exercise: List **2 tasks to automate** per hustle.

Month 4 – Expansion & Marketing:

- Promote your hustles to **new audiences**.
- Experiment with **low-cost marketing strategies** (social media, referrals, collaborations).
- Exercise: Set **3 marketing experiments** for the month.

Month 5 – Monetization & Scaling:

- Introduce **higher-value offerings** (packages, bundles, upsells).
- Diversify income within each hustle (freelance → course, content → affiliate).
- Exercise: Plan **1 new revenue stream** for each hustle.

Month 6 – Review & Optimize:

- Reflect on **progress, failures, and lessons learned**.
- Optimize workflows, automate more tasks, and scale the highest-

performing hustle.

- Exercise: Write a **summary of your progress**, including income, habits, and mindset growth.

2. Weekly Action Planner

To stay consistent, break each month into weekly goals:

Week Focus Actions Reflection

1. Setup. Choose primary hustle, tools, schedule. What is my biggest obstacle this week?

2. Skill-building. Learn 1 new skill related to hustle. What did I improve?

3. First outreach. Contact 5–10 clients/customers. What worked & what didn't?

4. Reflection. Track earnings & progress. Adjust next month's plan

Tip: Each week, dedicate **1 hour for planning and reflection**, even if your hustles only require 1–2 hours/day. Consistency beats intensity.

3. Daily Habit Tracker

Daily consistency is key to compounding success. Track:

- Hustle hours worked
- Tasks completed

- Income earned
- Lessons learned

Exercise: Create a **daily log template** like this:

Date
Hustle
Hours
Task Completed
Income
Notes/Lessons

4. Accountability & Support

Growth accelerates when you **share your progress and seek mentorship**:

- Join **online communities** of hustlers.
- Find **an accountability partner** for weekly check-ins.
- Seek **feedback on your work** to improve faster.

Personal Note:

I had an accountability partner during my first 6 months of side hustles. The weekly check-ins helped me **stay consistent and motivated**, even on low-income weeks. It's a small action that compounds massively over time.

5. Tracking Income & Growth

Set up **simple tracking sheets**:

- **Primary hustle income**
- **Secondary hustle income**
- **Passive or semi-passive income**
- **Total monthly income**

Exercise: Fill in **your income goal per hustle for each month**, even if it starts small.

Month. Primary Hustle. Secondary Hustle. Passive Income. Total Goal

1. ₹5,000 ₹2,000 ₹0 ₹7,000

2 ₹10,000 ₹4,000 ₹0 ₹14,000

…. … … …. …

6. Reflection & Mindset

Every month, answer:

1. What worked well?
2. What didn't?
3. What can I do differently next month?
4. Did I stay consistent with habits and hustles?
5. How am I feeling about my progress and mindset?

Tip: Celebrate **small wins**, because consistent progress beats one-time big wins.

7. Bonus Exercise: Your 6-Month Hustle Blueprint

Create your own visual blueprint using these sections:

- Hustle 1: Name → Goal → Action Steps → Revenue Target
- Hustle 2: Name → Goal → Action Steps → Revenue Target
- Passive Income: Name → Goal → Action Steps → Revenue Target

- Skills to learn each month
- People to connect with (mentors, collaborators, communities)

This becomes **your actionable, month-by-month plan** to implement everything you've learned in the book.

8. Key Takeaways

- **Consistency beats intensity**: Small daily actions compound into significant results.
- **Diversify income streams**: Protect yourself from risk and accelerate growth.
- **Plan and track**: Use weekly, monthly, and 6-month milestones.
- **Mindset is everything**: Confidence, accountability, and reflection fuel long-term success.
- **Action > Perfection**: Implement, test, learn, and scale.

By following this **6-month multi-hustle action plan**, you'll not only build income but also develop **the habits, mindset, and systems** to continue growing well beyond your first ₹10k/month.

39

Celebrating Your First Wins

"D*on't wait for opportunity. Create it."* – *Anonymous*

Have you ever wondered what it feels like to hold your first ₹10,000 earned entirely on your own? Not from your salary, not from your parents, not from luck—but from your ideas, effort, and persistence? That moment is electrifying. It's proof that you're capable of more than the 9-to-5 grind, proof that freedom is possible, proof that **your financial destiny is in your hands**.

I remember my first ₹10k vividly. I had been juggling a day job, freelancing late nights, sending countless proposals that went unanswered, and wondering if I was wasting my time. And then… it happened. A client said yes. The money landed in my account. My heart raced. I felt alive in a way I hadn't before. That wasn't just money—it was **validation**.

It told me: *I can do this. I can create my own income. I can break free from the ordinary.* And that's the first thrill of stepping into your own entrepreneurial journey.

Why Small Wins Are Huge

Most people dismiss small wins because they don't look like "real success." But here's the secret: **big results are built from small, repeated victories**.

After my first ₹10k, I didn't magically know how to make ₹1 lakh. But I knew I could replicate my efforts. I could improve, learn, and scale. That single win **changed my mindset**—from uncertainty to confidence. Every action afterward became easier because I had proof that I *could succeed.*

Mini Story:

My second client came just two weeks later. The difference? Confidence. I wasn't begging for work—I was showing value. That small shift in belief transformed my approach, my negotiations, and ultimately my income.

Identifying Your Wins

Wins aren't always monetary. They can be:

- Sending your first 20 proposals
- Learning a new skill for your side hustle
- Completing a small project
- Getting positive feedback or a referral

Exercise:
List 5 wins from the past 3 months—monetary or non-monetary. Reflect on how each one made you feel and what it taught you.

Celebrating wins, no matter how small, fuels momentum and motivation. Momentum is the hidden currency of success.

Confidence Through Reflection

Confidence isn't inherited; it's earned. I built mine by documenting every win. I'd ask myself:

1. What did I achieve?
2. How did it feel?
3. What can I do next?

These reflections helped me take bolder steps. My first ₹10k led to digital products, more clients, and eventually a small business—all because I acknowledged that **I was capable of growth**.

Mini Story:

After three months of consistent side hustle effort, I launched my first digital course. That first ₹10k win had proven that effort, persistence, and small wins compound into bigger outcomes. I wasn't just trading time for money anymore—I was leveraging skills and systems.

Turning Wins Into Action

A win without action is a memory. I learned to ask:

- What did I learn from this win?
- How can I scale it this month?
- What actionable step can I take this week?

Exercise:

Pick 1 recent win and write down:

- 3 ways to scale it in the next 30 days
- 1 specific action you'll take this week

The Compounding Effect

Consistency is your superpower. Even **1 hour/day** invested in your side hustle may feel small, but over 90 days, it builds skills, revenue, and momentum. Small wins compound like interest, not in your bank account, but in **your confidence, skillset, and income potential**.

Reflection

When I look back at my first ₹10k, it wasn't about money—it was about **belief**. That one win proved that I could challenge the middle-class trap, step out of comfort, and embrace calculated risks. Every win afterward became easier because the first proof existed.

Exercise

1. Reflect on **3 small wins** from the past 30 days.
2. For each win, write:

- What you learned
- How you can scale it this month
- One actionable step for this week

Takeaway

Small wins aren't just celebrations—they're **proof of capability, fuel for momentum, and the foundation of financial freedom**. Celebrate them, learn from them, and use them to scale toward your first big breakthrough.

40

Understanding Market Needs: Finding Your First Opportunity

"Opportunities don't happen. You create them." – *Chris Grosser*

Have you ever wondered why some people seem to effortlessly find work that pays well, while others struggle to even get a client? The truth is, success in side hustles isn't about luck—it's about understanding **what people truly need and are willing to pay for**. If you can spot opportunities that others ignore, you can build a business around solving real problems, not chasing random ideas.

When I started my first side hustle, I spent days asking myself: *What does the market want? Where is the gap I can fill?* I had skills in digital marketing, but skills alone weren't enough. I needed demand. That's when I learned the first unspoken rule of side hustles: **the market decides your success, not your passion alone**.

The Middle-Class Mindset vs. Opportunity Mindset

Many middle-class people are trained to play it safe: get a degree, secure a job, follow a predictable path. There's nothing wrong with that—but the problem arises when this mindset becomes a mental trap. Jobs offer security, but they also limit exposure to opportunities.

The difference between someone stuck in the 9-to-5 loop and a successful side hustler is market awareness. You have to stop thinking: "What can I do?" and start thinking: "What does the market need?"

In my first months, I tried to offer generic digital services—social media posts, website graphics—because I liked doing them. The results were discouraging. Only when I noticed local businesses struggling to generate leads online, and realized I could help them with simple, affordable campaigns, did I get my first paying clients. That insight changed everything. The lesson: the market tells you what's valuable.

How to Spot Opportunities Without Guesswork

Here's the approach I followed—and you can too:

1. **Listen to Complaints:** People constantly complain about problems. Those complaints are goldmines. For example, a friend of mine kept saying that small businesses had no time to manage their Instagram. That's a clear opportunity for social media management services.
2. **Observe Spending Patterns:** Where is money moving? If people are spending on tutoring, online courses, or niche products, there's demand. Your job is to figure out how to solve their pain or offer convenience.
3. **Identify Gaps in Existing Solutions:** Look at products or services in your area. What are they missing? Could you offer faster delivery, better service, or simpler solutions? Even small improvements can

generate revenue quickly.

4. **Test Your Ideas Quickly:** Don't spend months perfecting a product before checking if anyone wants it. I used free social media posts, a basic website, and simple proposals to validate my ideas. Within a week, I knew which services people were willing to pay for.

Exercise:

Take a notebook or digital document and write down **3 recurring problems or complaints** you've noticed in your personal or professional circles. For each problem, jot down **1 possible solution** you could offer.

Finding Your Niche Without Overthinking

Many beginners make the mistake of trying to serve everyone. That's the fastest way to overwhelm yourself and fail. A focused niche allows you to stand out, gain credibility, and deliver value efficiently.

For example, instead of offering "freelance marketing services for anyone," I specialized in **lead generation for local small businesses**. That focus made it easier for me to target clients, charge higher rates, and deliver measurable results.

A friend of mine tried to market to everyone—coaches, restaurants, online sellers, and local shops. He was exhausted and had little success. Once he narrowed to e-commerce stores selling handmade products, he doubled his clients in a month. Focus equals efficiency, clarity, and profitability.

Exercise:

Write down **3 niches or target audiences** where your skills or interests can solve a real problem. Next to each, describe **one problem they face** and **how you could solve it**.

Understanding Willingness to Pay

It's not enough for people to need something—they must be willing to pay for it. Here's a simple test I used in my first hustle:

- Approach 5–10 potential clients and **pitch your solution**.
- Observe reactions: Are they enthusiastic? Do they ask for pricing?
- Only move forward with solutions that people **pay for**, even small amounts.

I initially offered free services to build a portfolio. While I gained experience, I realized free work teaches nothing about **pricing, value, or client expectations**. When I asked clients to pay even a modest ₹500 for a simple task, suddenly my efforts felt real, clients respected my time, and I understood the value exchange.

Exercise:
Pick **one service or product** idea. Approach 5–10 people in your network and **ask if they'd pay for it**. Record responses. If at least 3–4 say yes, you're onto a viable idea.

Testing Demand Before Diving In

The fastest way to fail is to assume demand without testing. I learned this early: spending months developing services that no one wanted leads to burnout and wasted effort.
Steps to Test Quickly:

- Create a simple landing page or social media post describing your offer.
- Post it in communities where your audience hangs out.
- Collect feedback or small pre-orders.

This approach saved me months of wasted effort and helped me refine offers that **clients actually wanted to pay for**.

Reflection & Mindset Shift

The middle-class mindset teaches you to play safe. The side-hustle mindset teaches you to **listen, observe, and validate**. The key shift is:

- Stop guessing what might sell
- Start observing what people are already paying for
- Test, iterate, and improve

Exercise:

Reflect on the last 30 days:

1. What problems did you notice people complaining about?
2. How could you solve them?
3. Which solution could you test in the next 7–14 days?

Takeaways

- Opportunities are everywhere; you just need to **see them through a market lens**.
- Focus on **real problems people are willing to pay for**, not just what you enjoy.
- **Test ideas quickly** before committing time or money.
- Small, validated wins build confidence and momentum for your next side hustle steps.

Remember: A side hustle without demand is just a hobby. A side hustle with validated demand becomes your first step toward **financial freedom**.

41

Choosing Your First Side Hustle: From Idea to Action

"The best way to predict the future is to create it." – Peter Drucker

Have you ever felt stuck, knowing you want more from life, but unsure where to start? The truth is, many middle-class earners dream of financial freedom, but most never take the first step. Choosing your first side hustle can feel overwhelming because there are endless options. The key is **clarity, action, and testing**, not perfection.

When I first started, I spent weeks debating: Should I focus on freelancing? Should I create digital products? Should I try content creation? I wanted something that fit my skills, my schedule, and had paying customers waiting—but I didn't know where to start. The breakthrough came when I realized: **you don't have to be perfect, you just have to start**.

Why Starting Small Matters

Many beginners think they need a perfect, polished idea to succeed. This is the **illusion of perfection** that traps middle-class earners. In reality, starting small lets you **learn, adapt, and grow without risking too much**.

I remember launching my first freelance service with nothing more than a simple Google form to collect orders. It wasn't pretty. It wasn't "perfect." But within the first week, I landed two paying clients. Those small wins fueled my confidence and gave me **proof that I could actually make money outside a 9-to-5 job.**Starting small also allows you to **test your assumptions**. You might think people want fancy graphics, but maybe they actually just want simple, consistent social media posts. Only by starting small can you discover what truly sells.

Finding Your First Side Hustle

Here's how to identify your first opportunity:

1. **Look at Your Skills and Interests:**
2. Make a list of things you enjoy and skills you already have. Don't limit yourself—include anything from graphic design, writing, tutoring, to hobbies like photography or fitness coaching.
3. **Match Skills to Market Needs:**
4. Refer back to Chapter 2: what problems do people in your potential market have that you could solve? For example, if you're skilled at Excel, you could offer spreadsheet optimization services for small businesses.
5. **Pick Something Actionable:**
6. Avoid ideas that require massive upfront investment or years of learning. Start with what you can offer **this week**, even if it's small.
7. **Validate Your Idea Quickly:**
8. Before spending weeks building your service or product, test it. Talk to 5–10 potential clients, post a social media poll, or offer a beta service at a small fee. The feedback will tell you if you're on the right path.

Exercise:

Write down your **top 5 skills or hobbies**. Next to each, note **one way it could solve someone's problem or provide value**. Circle the one that seems easiest to test this month.

Comparing Popular Side Hustles

Many beginners get paralyzed by choice. Let's break down common options and how they work:

- **Freelancing:** Offers fast cash flow and flexibility. Examples: writing, graphic design, social media management. Pros: Low cost, fast start. Cons: Income tied to hours.
- **Digital Products:** E-books, templates, online courses. Pros: Can generate passive income. Cons: Requires upfront effort and validation.
- **Content Creation:** YouTube, Instagram, blogs, newsletters. Pros: Builds brand authority, audience, and long-term income. Cons: Takes time to monetize.
- **Local Services:** Tutoring, small business support, event planning. Pros: Immediate market, tangible results. Cons: Limited scalability if done solo.

I initially tried freelancing and content creation simultaneously. Freelancing gave quick wins, while content creation slowly built an audience. By combining both, I learned **how to diversify income streams without overcomplicating**.

Exercise:

List 3 side hustle ideas from the above categories that fit your skills and interests. For each, write **one small action you can take this week to test it**.

Overcoming the Fear of Starting

Fear is the number one reason people never launch their first hustle. You may think: *"What if I fail? What if no one pays me?"*

Here's the mindset shift that changed everything for me: **failure is data, not defeat.** Every client rejection, every missed sale, teaches you something. When I started, my first proposal was rejected by three clients. Instead of giving up, I asked why. Their feedback helped me refine my pitch—and my fourth proposal landed ₹5,000 in revenue.

Exercise:
Write down **one fear** holding you back from starting. Next to it, write **one action that challenges that fear** this week. For example: fear of no clients → reach out to 3 potential clients.

Taking the First Step

The most important part of this chapter is action. By the end of this week:

- You should have **chosen your first side hustle**
- Tested it with at least **5 potential clients or users**
- Collected **feedback or first paying orders**

I remember feeling nervous sending my first service offer to a stranger on LinkedIn. I thought I'd be ignored—or worse, laughed at. But the client responded within hours, eager to pay. That first transaction changed my mindset forever: **I was capable, and the market valued my skills**.

Takeaways

- Perfection is the enemy of action. Start small, learn fast.
- Match your skills to market needs; focus on **solving real problems**.
- Validate ideas quickly with real potential clients.
- Fear is natural; action transforms fear into momentum.
- Your first side hustle is proof that you can earn outside a 9-to-5.

Exercise:

Create a simple action plan:

1. Choose your first side hustle.
2. Identify 5 potential clients or users.
3. Send your first offer this week.
4. Collect feedback and adjust your approach.

Remember: The first step is always the hardest. Once you take it, momentum starts to build, small wins compound, and the journey to financial freedom begins

42

Money Mindset & Reinvesting

"Don't let money run your life, let money help you run your life better." *– John Rampton*

Have you ever felt like no matter how much you earn, it's never enough? That paycheck disappears faster than you can track it, leaving you wondering why your bank balance never seems to grow. Most middle-class earners think: *"I earn, I save, I spend, repeat."* But here's the truth: **if you want to break free and create wealth, you must change the way you think about money—and how you use it to grow more money.**

When I first started my side hustles, I made a huge mistake: I treated every rupee I earned as instant spending money. I was thrilled with my first ₹5,000, but it vanished within a week. The lesson hit me hard: earning is just the first step; **reinvesting is what multiplies wealth**.

The Middle-Class Money Trap

Most middle-class earners are trapped in a cycle of "income → expense → debt → repeat."

- You work hard to earn more.

- You spend on comfort, gadgets, family expenses.
- You feel financially stuck despite earning more than before.

This happens because our society conditions us to think **money is meant for spending, not multiplying**. Savings alone won't make you rich—investments and reinvestments do.

I remember earning ₹15,000 from my first side hustle month. I was ecstatic. But I spent ₹10,000 immediately on gadgets and dining out. Only ₹5,000 remained, which I reluctantly reinvested in ads and tools. That reinvestment turned into ₹50,000 within two months. That's when I realized: **your money works only when you put it to work**.

Changing Your Money Mindset

A millionaire mindset doesn't mean hoarding cash or taking reckless risks. It's about:

1. **Seeing money as a tool** – to invest in growth, skills, and opportunities.
2. **Prioritizing reinvestment** – every rupee earned should either grow your business, acquire new skills, or expand your network.
3. **Tracking cash flow** – know where every rupee goes; don't let it vanish unnoticed.

Exercise:

Take a look at your last month's spending. Categorize each expense as:

- Essential (bills, groceries)
- Comfort (dining, shopping)
- Investment (courses, tools, ads)

Circle areas where you can **redirect money from comfort to investment**.

Reinvesting Wisely

Not all reinvestments are equal. Here's what worked for me:

1. **Tools & Tech:** Investing in productivity and automation tools early saved hours and multiplied revenue.
2. **Learning & Education:** Every course I bought in the first year returned at least 3x in value, because it helped me improve my side hustle skills.
3. **Marketing & Advertising:** My first ₹5,000 ad spend earned ₹25,000 in revenue—a 5x ROI.

I once hesitated to spend ₹2,000 on a small social media ad campaign. My inner voice said, *"What if I lose it?"* I went ahead anyway. Within days, I landed 3 clients worth ₹12,000 total. That taught me: **risking small amounts on calculated investments is the fastest way to scale income**.

Exercise:

List 3 ways you can reinvest this month's earnings into your side hustle or skills. Next to each, note the expected return or benefit.

Budgeting for Growth

A strong money mindset also means knowing **where to allocate your income**. Here's a simple framework I used:

- **50% Reinvestment:** Tools, marketing, courses, growth opportunities.
- **30% Personal Savings:** Emergency funds, retirement accounts.
- **20% Rewards & Comfort:** Small treats to stay motivated without guilt.

Even if you earn only ₹1,000, this allocation trains your mind to prioritize growth first, comfort second.

Exercise:

Apply the 50-30-20 rule to your next side hustle earnings. Track your progress for 30 days and adjust as needed.

From Small Wins to Compounding Wealth

Money reinvested intelligently grows exponentially. A ₹5,000 investment can become ₹50,000 if done strategically. The key is **patience, consistency, and learning from feedback**.

I started with ₹1,000 investing in ads for a small content service. Month 1: earned ₹2,500. Month 2: reinvested ₹1,500 → earned ₹6,000. Month 3: reinvested ₹3,000 → earned ₹15,000. That simple compounding mindset **turned small wins into financial momentum**, proving that consistent reinvestment beats instant gratification every time.

Takeaways

- Treat money as a tool, not a reward.
- Prioritize reinvestment in skills, tools, and marketing.
- Track every rupee; redirect comfort spending into growth.
- Compounding small wins multiplies wealth faster than waiting for a big paycheck.
- Calculated risks with reinvestment lead to scalable income.

Exercise:

1. Look at your current income streams. How much can you reinvest this month?
2. List 3 reinvestment actions with expected outcomes.
3. Commit to executing **at least one reinvestment action within** 7 **days**.

Remember: Money doesn't create freedom by sitting idle—it grows when you use it smartly. The mindset of reinvestment separates earners from builders and is the cornerstone of financial independence.

43

Small Wins Build Confidence

"Success is the sum of small efforts repeated day in and day out." – *Robert Collier*

Have you ever felt overwhelmed by the idea of building wealth? The dream of financial freedom can feel so far away, it almost paralyzes you. What if I told you that the key to breaking free isn't a massive leap, but **a series of small, intentional wins that build momentum**?

When I started my first side hustle, I imagined earning ₹50,000 in the first month. Reality hit: my first ₹1,000 felt like a miracle. But that first small win changed everything—it gave me **confidence, clarity, and the courage to scale**.

Why Small Wins Matter

Most beginners think wealth is created overnight—through a viral idea, a lucky investment, or a single big client. The truth is: **confidence compounds**. Each small success builds belief in yourself and your abilities.

Small wins:

1. **Validate your skills:** You see that your effort produces results.

2. **Build momentum:** One small success leads to another.
3. **Reduce fear:** Taking the first step becomes easier after a small victory.
4. **Create a growth mindset:** You start thinking in terms of opportunities instead of limitations.

I remember landing my first ₹2,000 client through freelance writing. It wasn't life-changing financially, but mentally, it was a game-changer. I realized: *"If I can do this, I can do more."* That confidence fueled my next efforts, turning one small project into multiple clients and eventually recurring income.

The Psychology Behind Small Wins

Science backs this up: **dopamine, the "feel-good" hormone, is triggered by accomplishment**—even small ones. Each success reinforces behavior, making you more motivated to take action again.

Most middle-class earners ignore small wins. They wait for perfection or a big break. That's why they stay trapped. The key is **celebrating progress, not perfection**.

How to Identify Small Wins

Small wins aren't random; they're deliberate steps toward a bigger goal. Ask yourself:

- What is the smallest action I can take today that moves me closer to financial growth?
- Can I secure my first client, create my first product, or launch my first ad campaign?
- Which small task will teach me the most and build confidence?

Exercise:

Write down 5 "small wins" you can achieve in the next 7 days. Examples:

1. Send proposals to 3 potential clients.
2. Launch your first social media post promoting your side hustle.
3. Research 1 new tool that can improve productivity.
4. Draft a simple pricing plan for your service.
5. Reinvest ₹500 into ads or a learning resource.

Next to each win, write the **expected outcome and lesson learned**.

Compounding Small Wins

Small wins don't just build confidence—they **compound over time** into meaningful results. Think of them as stepping stones across a river: one step may seem tiny, but cumulatively, they carry you to the other side.

Case Study:

Ravi, a freelancer I mentored, started with a ₹1,000 project. He reinvested half his earnings into learning a new skill. Within 3 months, he had completed 10 small projects, built a portfolio, and secured a ₹15,000 recurring client. None of this would have been possible if he ignored those first small wins.

Exercise:

For each small win you achieve this week, write a one-line reflection:

- What did I learn?
- How does this bring me closer to my financial goal?

Using Small Wins to Scale

Once you start accumulating small wins, the next step is **scaling them systematically**:

1. **Repeat successful actions:** Identify what works and do more of it.
2. **Reinvest earnings:** Use profits from small wins to fund bigger opportunities.
3. **Track results:** Keep a simple journal of actions, outcomes, and lessons.
4. **Celebrate milestones:** Don't wait for the "big win" to feel accomplished.

I once hesitated to pitch for multiple clients, fearing rejection. After landing my first ₹1,000 job, I realized the fear was mostly in my head. I pitched 5 more clients the next day and secured 3. Small wins gave me **momentum and belief in my own abilities**.

Takeaways

- Confidence is built one step at a time—small wins matter.
- Track progress, reflect on lessons, and celebrate achievements.
- Small wins compound into bigger opportunities and income.
- Reinvesting and scaling small wins accelerates growth.
- Fear diminishes as you consistently achieve manageable goals.

Exercise:

1. Choose **one small action per day** that moves your side hustle forward.
2. At the end of the week, list all completed actions and what you learned.
3. Identify **the one action** that created the biggest impact and plan to scale it next week.

Remember: Every millionaire started with small wins. Confidence, momentum, and growth all begin with **the courage to take the first step**. Your first ₹1,000, your first client, your first product—each is a victory worth celebrating.

44

Scaling Your Hustle

"Don't work for money, make money work for you." – *Robert Kiyosaki*

Have you ever wondered why some people's side hustles seem to explode while others barely grow? What separates a hobby-level hustle from a scalable income machine? The answer is **intentional scaling**—taking small wins, proven methods, and turning them into reliable, recurring income streams.

When I started my first small online business, I had one client and one product. By month three, I was juggling multiple projects. The secret wasn't working harder—it was **working smarter and building systems to grow sustainably**.

Why Scaling is the Game-Changer

Scaling your hustle isn't just about earning more money. It's about:

1. **Expanding your reach:** More clients, more customers, more visibility.
2. **Optimizing your time:** Systems allow you to earn without doubling your hours.

3. **Reinvesting strategically:** Use profits to fuel growth instead of spending immediately.
4. **Building credibility:** A side hustle that scales builds a reputation, which opens doors to bigger opportunities.

I remember taking on 10 clients manually at the start—responding to every email and invoice by hand. It was exhausting. Once I invested in automation tools, simple templates, and a structured workflow, I could handle 3x the clients with half the effort. That shift allowed me to reinvest time and energy into acquiring even more business.

Step 1: Identify What's Scalable

Not all tasks are worth scaling. Ask yourself:

- Which of my current activities generate the most income relative to effort?
- What can be standardized, automated, or delegated?
- Which products, services, or offerings have the highest growth potential?

Exercise:

Create a "Hustle Audit" list:

- Write down your current income streams.
- Note how much time each requires.
- Identify one area with high potential for scale.

Step 2: Systematize Your Hustle

Systems are the backbone of growth. Without them, growth is limited by your personal capacity.

Example Strategies:

1. **Templates & Checklists:** Standardize common tasks like proposals, emails, and delivery processes.
2. **Automation Tools:** Schedule posts, manage clients, and track revenue with simple, free, or low-cost tools.
3. **Delegation:** Outsource repetitive tasks like editing, social media posting, or administrative work.

Case Study:

Ankur, a content creator I follow, started with one YouTube video a week. By systematizing scripts, video editing, and publishing schedules, he scaled to producing 3 videos per week, growing views, subscribers, and revenue.

Exercise:

Pick **one repetitive task** in your side hustle this week. Plan **how you will automate, delegate, or systematize** it. Note potential time saved and impact on growth.

Step 3: Expand Your Offerings

Scaling often means diversifying within your niche. Once your first service or product is stable, consider:

- Upsells: Offer premium versions or additional services.
- Packages: Bundle multiple services together for higher value.
- Complementary Products: Launch products or services that align with your audience's needs.

My first freelance design service earned me ₹5,000/month. When I added a mini-course teaching my design techniques, I earned an additional ₹10,000 without adding extra client work. That small expansion doubled my monthly income.

Exercise:

Brainstorm **3 ways to expand or enhance your existing side hustle offerings**. Note potential earnings and resources needed.

Step 4: Reinvest Profits Strategically

Scaling isn't just about earning more; it's about **reinforcing growth**.

- Allocate a percentage to learning new skills.
- Invest in marketing, tools, or courses that increase efficiency.
- Consider partnerships or collaborations to access larger audiences.

Case Study:

Ravi, my mentee, reinvested ₹5,000 from his first freelancing month into an online course on social media marketing. Within 2 months, he landed 3 new clients who were willing to pay ₹15,000 each. That reinvestment directly multiplied his revenue.

Exercise:

Decide **how much of your first ₹5,000–₹10,000 revenue you will reinvest**. Write down exactly where it will go and why.

Step 5: Track, Analyze, and Improve

Scaling without tracking is guessing. Develop simple metrics:

- How much time per client/project?
- Revenue per task/product?
- Client satisfaction and repeat business?

Reflect monthly: What worked? What didn't? Adjust and optimize constantly.

Exercise:

Create a **Monthly Hustle Tracker**:

- Revenue earned
- Time spent
- Lessons learned
- Next month's focus

Takeaways

- Scaling is intentional; it requires focus on systems, offers, and reinvestment.
- Small wins are the foundation—compound them through smart strategies.
- Automate, delegate, and optimize to multiply your impact without burning out.
- Reinvest profits strategically to fuel sustainable growth.
- Track results to continuously refine your process.

Remember: Scaling doesn't mean doing everything yourself. It's about **working smarter, not harder**, and turning your small wins into a sustainable, growing income stream. Your first ₹10,000 is proof—you can reach ₹50,000, ₹1 lakh, and beyond if you follow these steps consistently.

Next Exercise:

1. List your current side hustle tasks.
2. Identify **one task to systematize or delegate**.
3. Plan **one new offer or upsell** to increase income.
4. Decide **how much revenue to reinvest** this month.
5. Track progress weekly and reflect on lessons.

45

Building Multiple Streams of Hustle Income

"Don't put all your eggs in one basket." – Warren Buffett

Have you ever wondered why some people seem to make money no matter what happens in the economy, while others struggle to survive? The secret is **multiple income streams**. Imagine your side hustle isn't just one path to money but **several paths that support each other**, creating a safety net and amplifying your earnings.

When I started scaling my first side hustle, I realized that relying solely on freelance clients was risky. Some months I earned ₹20,000, other months barely ₹5,000. That's when I started thinking: "How can I make money even when one income source slows down?" This mindset shift opened doors to multiple revenue streams—and consistent growth.

Why Multiple Streams Matter

Multiple income streams:

1. **Reduce Risk:** If one stream dips, others compensate.

2. **Accelerate Growth:** More streams mean more opportunities for reinvestment.
3. **Build Financial Security:** You're not dependent on one client, job, or platform.
4. **Leverage Skills:** Different streams often use overlapping skills, making growth easier.

When I launched my first freelance design service, I added **a mini-course teaching my techniques** and **affiliate partnerships recommending software I used**. Within months, my revenue wasn't coming from a single client but **3 different sources**, making my hustle more stable and predictable.

Step 1: Identify Potential Income Streams

Think about your current skills and audience. Some common beginner-friendly streams include:

- **Freelancing:** Writing, design, programming, marketing, consulting.
- **Digital Products:** Courses, templates, eBooks, mini-guides.
- **Affiliate Marketing:** Promoting tools, apps, or services you already use.
- **Service Packages:** Bundle consulting, coaching, or freelance work for higher value.
- **Content Monetization:** YouTube, blogging, podcasts, social media sponsorships.

Exercise:

Write down **5 potential income streams** you could realistically start in the next 3 months. Rank them by effort, cost, and potential revenue.

Step 2: Start Small, Stack Strategically

It's tempting to jump into multiple hustles at once, but that's a recipe for burnout. Start with **one primary income stream**, then layer additional streams gradually:

- **Primary Stream:** Your main side hustle that generates revenue first.
- **Secondary Stream:** Related income that leverages the same audience or skills.
- **Tertiary Stream:** Passive or semi-passive income like digital products or affiliate links.

I started with freelancing as my primary stream. Once it was stable, I added a mini-course as a secondary stream. Later, I promoted affiliate tools to my audience as a tertiary stream. Within a year, these three streams together **tripled my income** compared to freelancing alone.

Exercise:
Create a **3-level income stream plan** for your hustle: Primary, Secondary, and Tertiary. Note **how much time, effort, and investment** each requires.

Step 3: Mini Hustle Blueprints

Here are some **practical blueprints** to help you visualize multiple income streams:

Blueprint 1 – Freelance + Course Path

- Primary: Freelance service (₹5k–₹15k/month)
- Secondary: Mini-course teaching your skills (₹2k–₹10k/month)
- Tertiary: Affiliate tools used in your work (₹1k–₹5k/month)

Blueprint 2 – Content + Affiliate Path

- Primary: YouTube channel / Blog monetized via ads
- Secondary: Affiliate marketing for tools or apps
- Tertiary: Digital products or workshops

Blueprint 3 – Service Bundle Path

- Primary: Coaching / Consulting service
- Secondary: Group coaching / membership program
- Tertiary: Templates, checklists, or guides sold online

Exercise:
Pick **one blueprint that fits your skills**. Write down **your first 3 actionable steps** to implement it this month.

Step 4: Reinvest and Multiply

Multiple streams allow you to **reinvest profits strategically**:

- Upgrade tools and automation for efficiency.
- Take short courses to improve your skill set.
- Invest in marketing to reach a broader audience.
- Explore collaborations to create new streams faster.

Case Study:
Rina, a beginner freelancer I mentored, started with content writing. She added a mini-course teaching writing basics, and then affiliate tools she used for productivity. By reinvesting 30% of profits into online ads, she **tripled revenue in 4 months**, without increasing her working hours.

Exercise:
Decide **how much revenue from your first stream you will reinvest**

into building the next stream. Document **specific actions and timelines**.

Step 5: Time Management for Multiple Streams

Managing multiple income streams can be overwhelming. Use **time-blocking and batching** to stay focused:

- Allocate specific days for each income stream.
- Batch repetitive tasks to save time.
- Automate wherever possible to prevent burnout.

Exercise:
Create a **weekly time-block schedule** for your income streams. Ensure each stream has **dedicated focus hours** without overlapping.

Takeaways

- Multiple streams reduce risk and accelerate growth.
- Start small: one primary income stream, then layer secondary and tertiary streams.
- Use mini blueprints to structure your hustle growth.
- Reinvest profits strategically to scale faster.
- Manage time carefully to maintain consistency without burnout.

Remember: One stream can feed you; multiple streams can **transform your life**. Each small income adds up, and the combination will give you freedom, security, and exponential growth.

Next Exercise:

1. List 3 income streams you could realistically start this month.
2. Choose a blueprint and write your **first 3 action steps**.
3. Decide **how much revenue to reinvest** in building new streams.

Create a **time-block plan** for managing multiple streams efficiently

46

Networking & Collaboration

"Your network is your net worth." – Porter Gale

Have you ever felt like you're working hard on your side hustle but progress feels slow, and opportunities aren't coming? What if I told you that the fastest way to accelerate growth isn't just working harder—but **connecting with the right people**?

When I started my first side hustles, I thought I could do everything alone. I spent weeks perfecting a service offer, only to realize that **one strategic connection could have saved me months of trial and error**. That moment changed my perspective: success grows faster when you **collaborate, not just compete**.

Why Networking & Collaboration Matter

1. **Accelerates Learning:** Mentors and peers teach lessons you'd spend years figuring out alone.
2. **Opportunities Multiply:** Collaborators bring clients, partnerships, and joint ventures.
3. **Credibility Boost:** Being associated with experienced people builds trust with your audience.

4. **Idea Exchange:** Networking sparks ideas that grow your income streams faster.

I remember reaching out to a fellow freelancer who had built a six-figure consulting business. A single coffee chat gave me **insights that doubled my side hustle revenue within three months**. That one connection also led to collaborative projects that exposed me to new audiences.

Step 1: Identify Your Network

Your network isn't just high-profile mentors—it includes:

- **Peers:** People at the same hustle level for brainstorming and accountability.
- **Mentors:** Experienced individuals who guide and correct your mistakes.
- **Potential Clients:** Those who can pay for your services or products.
- **Collaborators:** People whose skills complement yours for joint projects.

Exercise:

List **10 people** in these categories you want to connect with this month. Include one actionable step for each (DM, email, LinkedIn message, or coffee chat).

Step 2: Build Genuine Relationships

Networking isn't about asking for favors—it's about **giving first**.

- Help peers solve problems.
- Share resources, tips, or contacts freely.
- Engage consistently through messages, social media comments, or collaboration offers.

I once helped a fellow side hustler optimize their website for free. A month later, they referred three clients to me. I realized that **giving before asking creates trust and multiplies opportunities**.

Exercise:

Identify **one person you can help this week** without expecting anything in return.

Step 3: Attend Events & Online Communities

Even if you're busy, you can expand your network without traveling:

- **Local workshops or meetups:** Meet peers and mentors in person.
- **Online communities:** Facebook groups, LinkedIn forums, Reddit subreddits, Discord channels.
- **Webinars & virtual events:** Learn and connect with experts worldwide.

Exercise:

Join **2 relevant online communities** this week and introduce yourself in a meaningful, value-added way.

Step 4: Collaboration for Growth

Collaboration can multiply your results faster than solo work:

- **Joint Projects:** Partner with someone who has complementary skills.
- **Guest Content / Podcast:** Share each other's audience to expand reach.
- **Mentorship / Accountability Partnerships:** Accelerate learning and consistency.

Case Study:

Ankur, a friend I met through a freelancer community, and I decided to co-create a digital course. Each of our audiences brought in **over ₹50,000 in combined sales within the first month**. This partnership accelerated our growth far faster than individual efforts.

Exercise:

Identify **one potential collaborator** and draft a **3-step plan to propose a small project or partnership** this month.

Step 5: Maintain & Nurture Relationships

Networking is not one-time; it's a long-term effort:

- Schedule check-ins with key contacts.
- Celebrate their wins publicly.
- Share resources, insights, or introductions regularly.

I still keep in touch with my first mentor from six years ago. Occasionally, I send him insights, celebrate his milestones, or ask for advice. That long-term relationship has brought **consistent referrals and business growth** over the years.

Exercise:

Pick **3 existing contacts** and send meaningful messages to **reconnect and add value** this week.

Key Takeaways

- Networking is **multiplicative**: one connection can open multiple doors.
- Give first, build trust, and provide value before asking for anything.
- Attend events, join communities, and proactively seek collaboration.
- Long-term relationships create **sustained business growth**.

Remember: Success rarely happens in isolation. The people you surround yourself with determine **how fast and far your side hustles can grow**. Your network is the ladder that lifts your hustle beyond limits.

Next Exercises:

1. List 10 people in your network categories (peers, mentors, clients, collaborators).
2. Take one step this week to **help someone** in your network.
3. Join 2 online communities and introduce yourself meaningfully.
4. Identify one collaboration opportunity and draft a proposal.

Reconnect with 3 existing contacts to add value

47

Mastering Multiple Side Hustles

"Don't put all your eggs in one basket—but know how to manage them all at once." – Unknown

Have you ever wondered how some people seem to effortlessly earn from multiple sources, while others struggle to grow just one? Could you be missing out on a bigger financial picture simply because you're focusing on a single hustle?

When I started my journey, I had only one freelance project. I worked late nights, weekends, and was proud to earn my first ₹10k. But I realized quickly that **one hustle can only take you so far**. Scaling required **multiple income streams, smart time management, and leveraging my growing network**.

Why Multiple Side Hustles Matter

1. **Income Diversification:** If one source slows, others keep cash flowing.
2. **Skill Expansion:** Each hustle teaches you new skills that benefit all others.
3. **Opportunity for Passive Income:** Some hustles can eventually run

with minimal attention.

4. **Faster Financial Independence:** Multiple streams accelerate wealth-building and reduce reliance on any single job.

After my first freelance gig stabilized, I started a small digital product alongside it. Then I explored affiliate income from tools I used daily. Within a year, **my income had multiplied 4x**, and I was finally feeling in control of my financial future.

Step 1: Evaluate Your Hustles

Not every hustle is worth scaling. Ask yourself:

- Does it have growth potential?
- Can I systematize or outsource parts of it?
- Will it complement my other hustles or compete for my time?

Exercise:

List **all current income sources** and rate them on potential growth, effort required, and synergy with other hustles. Decide which to **scale, maintain, or pause**.

Step 2: Prioritize & Schedule

Balancing multiple hustles is about **time allocation and focus**.

- Create a weekly schedule for each hustle.
- Dedicate prime hours to the hustle with highest ROI.
- Batch similar tasks across projects for efficiency.

Mini-Blueprint:

- Hustle A (highest revenue potential) → Morning focus 3x/week

- Hustle B (mid-term growth) → Evening 2x/week
- Hustle C (passive/affiliate) → Automate & check weekly

Exercise:

Draft a 7-**day time-block plan** for all your hustles. Include 1 hour daily for learning and networking.

Step 3: Leverage Your Network

Connections are multiplier forces for multiple hustles:

- Collaborators can help you manage tasks across hustles.
- Mentors can guide you to prioritize high-impact hustles.
- Peers can provide leads, referrals, and skill-sharing.

I once connected with a content creator through a networking event. They helped me market one of my digital products to a new audience. Simultaneously, I referred freelance clients to them. **Both of our hustles benefited, creating a win-win synergy**.

Exercise:

Identify **2 contacts from your network** who could help you scale or cross-promote any of your hustles. Reach out this week.

Step 4: Systems & Automation

The key to managing multiple hustles is **automation**:

- Use scheduling tools for social media and content.
- Automate invoicing and payments.
- Set reminders for follow-ups and deadlines.

When I started automating my affiliate promotions and client follow-ups,

I could focus more on growth strategies instead of repetitive tasks. This gave me **hours every week** to either start new hustles or scale existing ones.

Exercise:
List **3 processes in your hustles that can be automated or delegated**. Take one step this week to implement it.

Step 5: Measure, Reflect & Adjust

Scaling multiple hustles requires regular assessment:

- Track revenue, time spent, and growth for each hustle.
- Adjust focus if a project underperforms.
- Celebrate small wins to maintain motivation.

Mini-Checklist:

- Weekly review: Revenue, clients, progress
- Monthly reflection: ROI, synergy with other hustles
- Quarterly adjustment: Scale, pause, or pivot hustles

Exercise:
Set up a **simple tracking sheet or journal**. Review your hustles weekly and note what's working, what isn't, and what to improve.

Takeaways

- Multiple side hustles multiply your **learning, income, and opportunities**.
- Time management, prioritization, and automation are essential.
- Your network can accelerate growth and open doors you can't reach alone.

- Consistent tracking ensures you're scaling efficiently without burning out.

Remember: You don't need to do everything perfectly. You need to **do multiple things consistently, learn fast, and optimize smarter.** Your side hustles are the foundation for financial freedom—and the more strategically you stack them, the faster you climb.

Next Exercises:

1. List all your current and potential hustles with growth potential.
2. Time-block each hustle in a weekly plan.
3. Identify 2 network contacts to collaborate or cross-promote.
4. Automate or delegate at least 1 repetitive task this week.
5. Set up a weekly review system to measure progress and adjust.

48

Networking & Collaboration

"Your network is your net worth." – Porter Gale

Have you ever wondered why some side hustlers skyrocket while others stay stuck, even if they have similar skills? Could it be that **who you know** matters just as much as **what you know**?

Early in my journey, I tried to do everything alone—freelancing, content creation, small digital products. I worked hard but felt stuck. Then I realized: **building the right connections could accelerate my growth exponentially**. Once I started networking strategically, doors opened that I didn't even know existed—collaborations, referrals, and mentorship that helped me multiply my income.

Why Networking & Collaboration Matter

1. **Access to Opportunities:** Thc right contacts can lead to clients, partnerships, and new ventures.
2. **Knowledge & Mentorship:** Learning from experienced people reduces trial-and-error.
3. **Collaboration for Growth:** Joint projects or co-branded offerings expand reach.

4. **Accountability & Motivation:** Connecting with like-minded hustlers keeps you consistent and inspired.

I remember reaching out to a mid-level freelancer in my niche. Initially, it was just to exchange ideas, but that connection turned into a joint project that generated **₹50,000 in revenue in one month**—all because we combined our skills and audience.

Step 1: Identify Your Network Targets

Think about these groups:

- **Peers:** People hustling in similar fields.
- **Mentors:** Those ahead of you who can provide guidance.
- **Collaborators:** Individuals whose skills complement yours.
- **Potential Clients:** Decision-makers who need your services.

Exercise:

Write a list of **10 people** you want to connect with this month across these four groups. Include one sentence on **why connecting with each would be mutually beneficial**.

Step 2: Start with Value

Networking isn't about asking for favors—it's about giving first.

- Share insights, tips, or resources.
- Celebrate their wins publicly.
- Offer to collaborate or contribute without expecting immediate return.

I reached out to a content creator whose audience overlapped with mine. I offered a free mini-guide for their newsletter. That simple act of value led to a **joint webinar**, generating both exposure and revenue.

Exercise:
Identify **one person this week** to provide value to, whether through advice, content, or collaboration.

Step 3: Leverage Online Platforms

- **LinkedIn:** Build credibility and connect with professionals.
- **Instagram / YouTube:** Engage with creators and potential clients.
- **Freelance Communities:** Join forums, Slack groups, or Discord channels.

Mini-Blueprint:

- Spend 15–30 minutes daily commenting, sharing insights, or messaging peers.
- Participate in 1–2 online events or webinars per month.
- Keep track of connections and follow up consistently.

Exercise:
Create a **weekly networking schedule**: list the platforms, daily engagement actions, and follow-up reminders.

Step 4: Collaborate Strategically

Look for **win-win opportunities**:

- Co-create products or services.
- Host webinars or workshops together.
- Share each other's audience through content or promotions.

A collaboration with a freelancer complementing my skills brought in **3 new high-value clients** in one month. We split responsibilities, leveraged our audiences, and both earned more than we would have alone.

Exercise:

Draft a **Collaboration Plan**: list 3 potential partners, the type of collaboration, and one action step to approach them this week.

Step 5: Maintain & Nurture Relationships

- Follow up regularly.
- Celebrate their wins.
- Offer help whenever possible.

Tip: Treat relationships like a **garden**. Regular care produces long-term growth.

Exercise:

Pick **5 key connections** and write personalized messages this week—check-in, share an update, or offer value.

Key Takeaways

- Your network directly impacts your opportunities, growth, and revenue potential.
- Always lead with value before expecting anything in return.
- Collaborations amplify reach, trust, and credibility.
- Consistent follow-up and nurturing turn casual connections into long-term partnerships.

Remember: **Alone you can go fast, but together you can go far.** Building meaningful relationships is not optional—it's essential for multiplying your side hustle earnings and achieving financial freedom.

Next Exercises:

1. Make a **list of 10 people** you want to connect with this month.

2. Identify **one way to add value** to a connection this week.
3. Build a **weekly networking schedule** for engagement and follow-up.
4. Draft a **Collaboration Plan** with 3 potential partners.
5. Write personalized messages to **5 key connections** to nurture relationships.

This chapter naturally sets up **Chapter 13 – Mastering Multiple Side Hustles**, where readers will learn how to juggle and scale multiple income streams while leveraging the networks they've built.

49

Mastering Multiple Side Hustles

"Don't put all your eggs in one basket—but make sure each basket grows your wealth." –

Have you ever felt like one income stream just isn't enough? Maybe your first side hustle brought in ₹10k, but you worry: what if it stops tomorrow? What if the client disappears, or the market changes?

That's exactly what I felt early in my journey. I had a single freelancing gig, and while it gave me hope, it wasn't enough. I realized **to truly escape the middle-class trap, I needed multiple, complementary income streams**. That's when I began experimenting—freelancing, creating small digital products, and even affiliate partnerships. The learning curve was steep, but the growth and financial security were undeniable.

Why Multiple Hustles Matter

1. **Risk Mitigation:** If one income stream slows down, others keep flowing.
2. **Skill Diversification:** Different hustles teach different skills—marketing, sales, product creation.
3. **Accelerated Growth:** Combining revenue streams multiplies your

total earnings faster.

4. **Financial Freedom:** More income streams = faster reinvestment → faster scaling.

I started with a freelance copywriting gig. Within three months, I added a small online course based on my expertise. Then I joined an affiliate program in the same niche. Within six months, my total income was **triple what I earned from freelancing alone**, and I wasn't stressed about a single client leaving.

Step 1: Identify Complementary Side Hustles

Look for hustles that:

- **Use overlapping skills** (example: writing → copywriting, content creation, course).
- **Target similar audiences** (example: freelancers → offer coaching or templates).
- **Require manageable time investment** (so you don't burn out).

Exercise:
List **3 hustles** you could start this month. For each, write one line on how it complements your existing hustle.

Step 2: Time Allocation & Prioritization

Juggling multiple hustles requires **strategic time-blocking**.

- **Primary Hustle:** 50–60% focus—your main revenue driver.
- **Secondary Hustle:** 20–30%—complementary income.
- **Tertiary Hustle:** 10–20%—testing new opportunities.

Personal Tip:

I blocked **1 hour per day** for my secondary hustle and **2 hours on weekends** for my tertiary experiments. Within two months, the tertiary hustle became a secondary income stream.

Exercise:
Create a **weekly schedule** allocating hours for each hustle. Include specific tasks for each block.

Step 3: Reinvest Wisely

Every additional hustle generates money—don't spend it all immediately.

- Reinvest in **skills** (courses, tools).
- Reinvest in **marketing** (ads, promotions).
- Reinvest in **automation tools** to save time.

After earning ₹15k from my first two side hustles, I invested ₹5k into an email automation tool. Within a month, it generated ₹20k in recurring sales—more than doubling my investment.

Exercise:
Identify **one expense this month** that will help scale any of your hustles.

Step 4: Systems & Automation

Multiple income streams can get messy without systems.

- **Task Lists & Calendar:** Track deadlines and commitments.
- **Automation Tools:** Email sequences, payment collection, social posting.
- **Templates:** Standardize repetitive tasks for faster execution.

Exercise:

Create a **system checklist** for each hustle: list the tasks, tools, and recurring processes.

Step 5: Collaboration & Outsourcing

Leverage other people's skills to scale faster:

- **Freelancers:** Delegate tasks that drain your energy.
- **Partners:** Co-create content, products, or marketing campaigns.
- **Mentors:** Seek advice on scaling strategies.

I hired a virtual assistant to handle client onboarding for one hustle. This freed 10 hours a week, which I used to develop a second digital product. Within three months, revenue from both streams **doubled**.

Exercise:
List **one task per hustle** you could delegate this month and identify potential collaborators.

Key Takeaways

- Multiple side hustles reduce risk and accelerate income growth.
- Focus on complementary hustles that align with your skills and audience.
- Reinvest profits strategically to scale faster.
- Systems, automation, and delegation are essential for managing multiple streams.

Remember: **Your first hustle is just the beginning. Each additional stream multiplies your earning potential and brings you closer to true financial freedom.**

Next Exercises:

1. Identify **3 complementary hustles** you can start.
2. Create a **weekly time-block schedule** for all hustles.
3. Plan one **reinvestment** for scaling.
4. Build a **system checklist** for each hustle.
5. List **tasks to delegate or collaborate** this month.

50

Building Your Personal Brand

"Your brand is what people say about you when you're not in the room."
– Jeff Bezos

Have you ever wondered why some freelancers, side hustlers, or entrepreneurs seem to attract clients effortlessly while others struggle? The answer is simple: **they have a personal brand that commands attention and trust.**

When I first started my side hustles, I treated every project as just a transaction. I thought, "If I deliver good work, people will come." But I learned quickly—without a **brand**, I was invisible in a sea of competitors. That's when I shifted my focus: I started sharing my journey, my insights, and my expertise publicly. Within months, people began reaching out to me, clients trusted me faster, and opportunities multiplied.

Why Personal Branding Matters

1. **Credibility & Trust:** A clear brand makes people confident in working with you.
2. **Visibility & Recognition:** When your audience knows your name, skills, and values, you stand out.

3. **Premium Pricing:** People pay more for someone they perceive as an expert.
4. **Opportunities Multiply:** Partnerships, collaborations, speaking gigs, and higher-paying clients come naturally.

I once had a small digital product that barely sold. After I shared a story on LinkedIn about my struggles and solutions, it sold out in 24 hours. My personal brand—my story—became the magnet for sales.

Step 1: Define Your Unique Value

Ask yourself:

- What am I known for?
- What problem do I solve better than anyone else?
- What values do I want my audience to associate with me?

Exercise:
Write a **personal brand statement** in one sentence. Example:
"I help freelancers build recurring income streams by teaching practical, actionable strategies they can implement today."

Step 2: Choose Your Platforms

You don't need to be everywhere—focus on where your audience spends time.

- **LinkedIn:** Ideal for freelancers and B2B services.
- **Instagram / YouTube:** Great for storytelling, content creation, and digital products.
- **Blogs / Medium:** Position yourself as a thought leader.
- **Email Newsletter:** Direct connection with your audience.

Personal Tip:

I started with LinkedIn and email because my target clients were professionals and small business owners. Consistency was key—posting 3–4 times per week and sharing actionable insights built trust fast.

Exercise:

Select **2–3 platforms** to focus on. Commit to posting at least **once per week** for the next month.

Step 3: Share Your Story

People connect with stories, not sales pitches.

- Share **journeys**, including struggles and lessons learned.
- Share **wins**, even small ones—they inspire others.
- Share **insights**, tips, and actionable advice.

I once shared a post about my first ₹1,000 side hustle milestone and the mistakes I made. The engagement was massive, and several readers became clients because they trusted me from my story.

Exercise:

Write **one story post** that shares a personal lesson or success from your side hustle.

Step 4: Position Yourself as an Expert

- Teach, don't sell—educate your audience.
- Offer free tips, templates, or insights to build credibility.
- Share results from your work to demonstrate authority.

Personal Tip:

I created a small "Side Hustle Starter Kit" PDF. I gave it away for free, and it established my authority. People trusted me enough to buy my first paid course shortly after.

Exercise:
Create **one piece of free value** (PDF, checklist, video) you can share with your audience this month.

Step 5: Consistency is Key

A personal brand is like a plant—it grows slowly and needs daily attention.

- Post regularly.
- Engage with comments and messages.
- Maintain your brand voice and values consistently.

Consistency made all the difference. I posted for six months almost daily before seeing tangible results. By month seven, leads were coming without me chasing clients.

Exercise:
Set a **3-month posting schedule** for your chosen platforms. Include content ideas, post type, and frequency.

Key Takeaways

- Your personal brand is your silent salesperson.
- Storytelling builds connection, credibility, and trust.
- Focus on platforms that reach your target audience.
- Consistency, free value, and expertise amplify your reach.

Remember: **Your personal brand is not just your logo or color scheme—it's the reputation, trust, and value you consistently provide.**

Next Exercises:

1. Define your **personal brand statement**.
2. Choose **2–3 platforms** to focus on.
3. Share **one personal story post** this week.
4. Create **one free value asset** to build authority.
5. Plan a **3-month content schedule** for consistency.

51

Scaling Your Network & Collaborations

"Your network is your net worth." – Porter Gale

Have you ever wondered why some people seem to attract opportunities effortlessly, while others work hard yet stay stuck? The secret often isn't just skill—it's **who you know and how you connect.**

When I first started my side hustles, I focused solely on delivering work. I ignored building relationships, thinking results alone would speak for themselves. Big mistake. I learned that even a brilliant skill can remain unnoticed without a **network of the right people**.

Why Networking Matters

1. **Opportunities Multiply:** Collaborations, partnerships, and referrals come from the people you know.
2. **Learning & Growth:** Surrounding yourself with like-minded individuals accelerates your skills and insights.
3. **Trust & Credibility:** When respected peers endorse you, your credibility skyrockets.
4. **Scale Faster:** With the right collaborations, you can achieve results that would take years alone.

I met a fellow freelancer at a local meet-up. We started collaborating on small projects. Within six months, our combined efforts landed us clients that individually we could never have reached. That collaboration became a consistent income stream and even led to a joint course launch.

Step 1: Identify Your Network Targets

Ask yourself:

- Who can teach me new skills?
- Who can refer clients or opportunities?
- Who could I collaborate with for mutual growth?

Exercise:
Create a **list of 10 people** you admire or could learn from. Include peers, potential mentors, and collaborators. Note down how you could approach them this month.

Step 2: Give Before You Receive

Networking is not about asking for favors immediately—it's about **providing value first**.

- Share knowledge freely.
- Promote other people's work.
- Offer help without expecting instant return.

Personal Tip:
I helped a colleague with free social media guidance. Six months later, they referred me to their client, which became my first ₹50,000 side project. Giving first builds goodwill and long-term partnerships.

Exercise:

Identify **one person in your list** and offer help, advice, or a collaboration this week.

Step 3: Build Meaningful Collaborations

Collaboration amplifies results:

- **Joint Projects:** Combine expertise for higher value offerings.
- **Cross-Promotion:** Share each other's content or products to reach new audiences.
- **Learning Partnerships:** Partner with someone to skill-up faster.

I partnered with a content creator to bundle our services. Our combined offer was more attractive, and we landed a client willing to pay **double** what I usually charged. Collaboration multiplied revenue without doubling work.

Exercise:

Draft **one potential collaboration plan** with a peer or expert in your field. Include steps, roles, and timeline.

Step 4: Attend Events & Online Communities

Your environment shapes your network:

- **Local meet-ups & workshops:** Ideal for making in-person connections.
- **Online forums & LinkedIn groups:** Expand reach and engage with experts.
- **Masterminds / Peer groups:** Surround yourself with ambitious peers.

Personal Tip:

Joining a small online mastermind group changed everything for me. The ideas, accountability, and connections accelerated my side hustle growth far faster than working alone.

Exercise:
Join **one relevant online group** or attend a local event this month. Set a goal to **connect with 3 new people** at each event.

Step 5: Keep Nurturing Relationships

Networking isn't a one-time effort—it's an ongoing process.

- Follow up with your contacts regularly.
- Share your wins and insights.
- Celebrate others' achievements.

I maintain a simple monthly email to my key contacts sharing updates, lessons, or helpful tips. It keeps me top-of-mind, and several opportunities came from people remembering me because of this small habit.

Exercise:
Create a **relationship map** of your contacts and schedule **monthly touchpoints** to nurture them.

Key Takeaways

- Your network can accelerate opportunities, learning, and revenue.
- Give before expecting return; provide value first.
- Collaborate strategically to multiply results.
- Attend events, join communities, and nurture relationships consistently.

Remember: **It's not about collecting contacts—it's about cultivating meaningful relationships that lead to growth, opportunities, and**

financial freedom.

Next Exercises:

1. List 10 potential mentors, peers, or collaborators.
2. Offer help to at least 1 person on your list.
3. Draft a collaboration plan with a peer.
4. Join 1 online community or attend 1 event.
5. Create a monthly relationship nurturing schedule.

52

Monetizing Your Brand & Network

"Your brand is your promise; your network is your leverage."

Have you ever wondered why some people effortlessly convert attention into income while others struggle to monetize even a loyal following? The secret lies in **knowing your value, leveraging relationships, and creating offers people can't resist.**

I learned this the hard way. When I first started sharing my knowledge online, I had a growing audience, friends in the industry, and even some repeat clients—but I struggled to turn these connections into consistent revenue. Everything changed when I realized **monetization isn't about selling—it's about structuring offers, building trust, and providing real value.**

Step 1: Define Your Value Proposition

Before monetizing your network, you need clarity on **what you offer**:

- What problems can you solve for your audience?
- What unique skills or experiences set you apart?
- How can your network benefit from collaborating with you?

I had skills in digital marketing and a growing network of freelancers. Instead of pitching random services, I packaged my expertise into a **consultation + mini-course bundle**, offering a clear solution for businesses needing fast growth. The result? Within two months, my first ₹50,000 project came from a referral.

Exercise:

Write down **3 core problems** you solve. Next, define **how your network can benefit** if they collaborate with or hire you.

Step 2: Package Offers for Different Segments

Not everyone in your network has the same needs or budget. Structuring **tiered offerings** can help you monetize efficiently:

1. **Low-ticket offers:** Short workshops, eBooks, or mini-services.
2. **Mid-ticket offers:** Monthly subscriptions, consulting sessions, or bundled services.
3. **High-ticket offers:** Premium coaching, joint ventures, or long-term retainers.

Personal Tip:

I started with small, affordable consulting sessions for beginners in my field. Those who got results upgraded to higher-tier packages. This tiered approach allowed me to monetize without overwhelming my audience.

Exercise:

Create **1 low-ticket, 1 mid-ticket, and 1 high-ticket offer** based on your skills and network.

Step 3: Leverage Collaborations for Revenue

Your network isn't just for advice—it can **actively generate income** through collaborations:

- **Joint offers:** Partner with a peer to sell a combined product or service.
- **Affiliate collaborations:** Promote others' services for a commission.
- **Referral programs:** Incentivize network connections to refer clients.

I partnered with a content creator to offer a "Brand + Marketing Bundle." Our audiences overlapped but were not identical. The bundle sold out in the first week, generating revenue neither of us could have achieved alone.

Exercise:

Identify **1 potential partner** in your network and draft a **collaboration proposal** that benefits both parties financially.

Step 4: Build a Monetization Funnel

Turning attention into income requires a **simple system**:

1. **Attract:** Share valuable content consistently.
2. **Engage:** Build trust through interactions, comments, and personal messages.
3. **Offer:** Present products or services that solve specific problems.
4. **Deliver:** Provide excellent results to encourage referrals and repeat business.

Personal Tip:

I created a mini funnel using my network: social media posts → free consultation → paid mini-course. Even without paid ads, my first ₹1,00,000 came purely from my connections and network trust.

Exercise:

Sketch a **3-step funnel** for monetizing your personal brand using your network: attract → engage → offer.

Step 5: Continuous Value Creation

Monetization isn't a one-time act; it's an ongoing process:

- Keep educating and inspiring your network.
- Provide results first; selling comes naturally afterward.
- Collect feedback to improve your offers.

After delivering a successful consulting project, I stayed in touch with clients, shared updates, and offered advanced solutions. Many returned for higher-ticket services, and several referred me to their network. Continuous value turned initial income into recurring revenue.

Exercise:

Create a **3-month content & engagement plan** for your network. Include tips, advice, and small offers that maintain trust while opening monetization opportunities.

Key Takeaways

- Monetization starts with clarity on your **unique value**.
- Tiered offerings help serve multiple audience segments effectively.
- Collaborations multiply revenue without multiplying effort.
- A simple funnel converts attention into consistent income.
- Continuous value creation ensures long-term monetization and trust.

Remember: **Your brand and network are your most powerful assets. Monetize ethically, provide real value, and your income will naturally follow.**

Next Exercises:

1. Define 3 problems you solve and how your network benefits.
2. Create a low, mid, and high-ticket offer.
3. Draft 1 collaboration proposal.
4. Sketch a monetization funnel for your personal brand.
5. Plan a 3-month engagement strategy to provide value and maintain monetization.

53

Automating Your Hustle

"Work smarter, not harder, and let your systems do the heavy lifting."

Have you ever felt like you're spinning your wheels, working endless hours on your side hustle but never seeing the freedom or growth you imagined? What if I told you that the same hustle could earn more **while you sleep**, simply by setting up the right systems?

When I started juggling multiple side hustles, I realized that **time is finite, but money can scale infinitely**—if you automate smartly. At first, I tried doing everything myself—emails, client onboarding, payments, follow-ups—and it was exhausting. That's when I discovered the true power of **automation**.

Step 1: Identify Repetitive Tasks

Automation starts by spotting tasks that **repeat daily or weekly**:

- Responding to emails or inquiries
- Client onboarding and follow-up
- Social media posting
- Payment collection

- Delivering digital products

In my first freelance venture, I spent 10–15 hours a week sending emails and scheduling calls. Once I automated follow-ups and appointment bookings, I freed 8 hours weekly—hours I reinvested in creating new offerings. That alone increased my revenue by 20% in the first month.

Exercise:
List 5 tasks in your side hustle that **repeat weekly or monthly**. Highlight the ones that **consume the most time**.

Step 2: Choose Simple Tools

You don't need complex systems to start automating:

- **Email Automation:** MailerLite, ConvertKit, or Gmail auto-responders
- **Scheduling Tools:** Calendly or Google Calendar
- **Payment & Delivery:** Razorpay, PayPal, or Gumroad
- **Social Media Scheduling:** Buffer, Hootsuite, or Canva Scheduler

Personal Tip:
I started with MailerLite for email sequences and Calendly for appointments. I didn't buy expensive software; I started with **tools that were free or low-cost**, then scaled as my revenue grew.

Exercise:
Pick **2 automation tools** you can implement this month. Write down **what task each tool will automate**.

Step 3: Create Standardized Processes

Automation isn't just tools; it's **processes that can run themselves**:

1. Define your workflow step-by-step.
2. Identify where technology or templates can replace manual effort.
3. Test and refine until the system works reliably.

For one of my digital courses, I created a **standard onboarding workflow**: purchase → automated welcome email → access to course → follow-up email for feedback. Once set, it ran smoothly without me lifting a finger, while students felt personally guided.

Exercise:

Write a **step-by-step process for one part of your hustle** (e.g., client onboarding, delivering a service, or content distribution) and mark steps you can automate.

Step 4: Automate Marketing & Sales

Your hustle doesn't grow if you rely solely on manual outreach. Automation in marketing is a game-changer:

- **Email Sequences:** Nurture leads automatically over time
- **Social Media Automation:** Schedule posts, stories, or tweets in advance
- **Sales Funnels:** Pre-designed funnels can convert leads into paying clients while you focus on creating new offers

I once launched a mini-course using a pre-built funnel. Leads signed up, got automated emails, and purchased without me interacting directly. The first launch earned ₹80,000 while I spent that week working on a new project.

Exercise:

Draft a **mini marketing funnel** you can automate within the next 30 days. Include lead capture, automated emails, and a simple offer.

Step 5: Delegate & Outsource

Automation is not just tech—it's also **leveraging people**:

- Hire virtual assistants for repetitive tasks
- Use freelancers for content creation or editing
- Delegate customer support with scripts or chatbots

When my freelance workload doubled, I hired a VA for customer queries. By training them on scripts and templates, they handled 80% of tasks I used to do. That freed my time to develop high-ticket offers, tripling my revenue in six months.

Exercise:

List **1 task you can outsource this month**, write a clear instruction sheet, and research a freelancer or VA platform.

Step 6: Measure & Optimize

Automation isn't "set and forget." You need **tracking and tweaking**:

- Monitor key metrics: sales, leads, and engagement
- Track time saved and tasks completed automatically
- Adjust sequences, workflows, and offers to improve conversions

I automated my email campaigns, but after 2 months, open rates dropped. I analyzed the sequence, tweaked subject lines and messaging, and saw engagement spike by 30%. Systems work best when continuously refined.

Exercise:

Choose **1 automated process** and define **3 KPIs to track success** this month.

Key Takeaways

- Identify repetitive tasks and automate them first.
- Start with simple, low-cost tools before scaling.
- Standardized processes make your hustle scalable.
- Automation can handle marketing, sales, and delivery.
- Delegate repetitive tasks to free your time.
- Track, analyze, and refine constantly.

Remember: **Automation doesn't remove the need for effort—it multiplies it. Set up smart systems, and watch your hustle grow while you focus on what matters most.**

Next Exercises:

1. List 5 repetitive tasks and choose 2 to automate immediately.
2. Select 2 tools to implement this month.
3. Create a step-by-step process for one core task and mark automation points.
4. Draft a mini automated marketing funnel.
5. Identify 1 task to outsource and create clear instructions.
6. Define 3 KPIs for one automated process to track improvements.

54

Scaling & Leveraging Your Hustle Network

"Your network is your net worth." – Porter Gale

Have you ever wondered why some side hustlers seem to explode overnight while others struggle to gain traction despite working equally hard? The secret often isn't more hours—it's **who you know, how you connect, and how you leverage your network**.

When I first started my side hustles, I thought I had to do everything myself. I hustled, created, marketed, and sold alone. Months passed, and growth felt slow. Then I realized: **the right connections could accelerate everything**—more clients, more referrals, and even collaborative opportunities I hadn't imagined.

Step 1: Map Your Current Network

Begin by understanding your starting point. Your current network includes:

- Friends and family
- Colleagues and former classmates

- Social media connections
- Communities, forums, or clubs you participate in

I once reached out to a college friend I hadn't spoken to in years. A simple "Hey, I'm building a digital course, do you know anyone who might benefit?" turned into my **first 5 paying clients**. That moment taught me: **you don't need a huge network; you need the right outreach.**

Exercise:

Write down 10 people in your current network who could help you grow your side hustle. Include their contact info and how you might reach out.

Step 2: Expand Strategically

Your goal is **quality over quantity**. Focus on connections that:

- Align with your niche
- Complement your skills
- Could provide mentorship or collaboration opportunities

I joined a small online community of freelance coaches. By engaging consistently, sharing value, and helping others, I landed **3 collaborations** that generated ₹50,000 in extra revenue over two months.

Exercise:

Identify 3 online or offline communities that align with your hustle. Plan to **engage actively for at least 30 minutes a day** for the next week.

Step 3: Build Mutually Beneficial Relationships

Networking isn't asking for favors; it's about creating **win-win situations**. Think:

- What value can you provide before asking for anything?
- How can collaboration help both parties grow?

I offered to guest post for another freelancer's blog in exchange for exposure to their audience. That single post brought **over 200 potential leads** and 2 new clients. By giving first, I received much more than I expected.

Exercise:
List 3 ways you can **add value to someone in your network** this month without asking for anything in return.

Step 4: Leverage Referrals & Testimonials

Referrals are **one of the fastest ways to scale**:

- Ask happy clients for introductions
- Encourage reviews and testimonials
- Offer referral incentives when appropriate

After completing a project for one client, I casually asked, "Do you know anyone else who might benefit?" That single referral turned into **a recurring project worth ₹30,000/month**. Testimonials on my social media also attracted inquiries without me chasing clients.

Exercise:
Draft a **referral request script** or testimonial request template you can send to your next 5 satisfied clients.

Step 5: Collaborate Strategically

Collaborations multiply reach and credibility:

- Co-create content with peers

- Launch joint offers
- Partner for webinars or workshops

I co-hosted a webinar with a content creator in a complementary niche. Our combined audience **doubled registration**, and I gained **10 high-ticket clients** in one week. Collaboration didn't just increase revenue; it increased my **credibility and authority**.

Exercise:
List 2 potential collaborators in your niche. Plan **one joint project** you could execute in the next 60 days.

Step 6: Track & Scale Your Network

Just like your side hustle, your network requires strategy:

- Track outreach: messages sent, follow-ups, collaborations initiated
- Review results: new clients, opportunities, partnerships
- Double down on high-impact relationships

I kept a simple Google Sheet tracking every outreach effort. After three months, I realized **20% of my contacts were producing 80% of results**. I focused on nurturing these high-value relationships and scaled my business faster than ever.

Exercise:
Create a simple **network tracking sheet**. Include name, contact, relationship type, last interaction, and potential opportunities. Review weekly.

Key Takeaways

- Map your existing network and understand its potential.
- Expand strategically with quality connections.
- Provide value first; networking is a two-way street.
- Leverage referrals, testimonials, and collaborations.
- Track and focus on high-impact relationships.

Remember: **Your network is a living ecosystem. Nurture it, leverage it wisely, and it will multiply your income, opportunities, and freedom.**

Next Exercises:

1. List 10 people in your current network and plan outreach.
2. Identify 3 communities to engage with for growth.
3. List 3 ways to add value to someone this month.
4. Draft referral/testimonial request templates.
5. Identify 2 potential collaborators and plan a joint project.
6. Track outreach and results using a simple sheet.

55

Monetizing Your Brand & Network

"You don't get paid for what you know, you get paid for what you share." – Robin Sharma

Have you ever felt that building a brand and networking is exciting—but you're not quite sure **how to turn it into real income**? Many side hustlers invest hours in content creation, community engagement, and collaboration, yet revenue doesn't follow. The secret lies in **strategically monetizing your brand and network** without feeling pushy or salesy.

When I started, I struggled with this. I had a small, engaged following online, clients loved my work, and opportunities came knocking—but I didn't know **how to convert attention into sustainable income**. Over time, I discovered the power of structured monetization, and it transformed my side hustles into real, recurring revenue streams.

Step 1: Identify Your Monetization Paths

Every brand has multiple ways to monetize:

- **Products:** digital courses, eBooks, guides
- **Services:** coaching, consulting, freelancing

- **Affiliate partnerships:** promoting products you believe in
- **Events & workshops:** webinars, paid live sessions
- **Sponsored content:** collaborations with brands

I began monetizing my brand with **freelancing and small workshops**. Soon, I added an eBook and online course, creating **three simultaneous income streams**. By diversifying, I avoided dependency on a single revenue source and increased total income by 5x in 6 months.

Exercise:
List **all possible ways you could monetize your brand or network**. Highlight at least 2 that you can implement within the next 30 days.

Step 2: Packaging Your Offer

The way you **present your product or service** determines its value perception:

- Bundle small wins into higher-value packages
- Offer tiered pricing for beginners → intermediate → advanced users
- Add bonuses to increase perceived value

I created a **3-tier online course package**: Basic (self-study), Premium (with live Q&A), and Elite (personal coaching). This simple structure allowed clients to choose their comfort level while maximizing my revenue from the same audience.

Exercise:
Take your product/service idea and **draft a 3-tier offer** with clear benefits for each level.

Step 3: Leveraging Your Network

Your connections are one of the fastest paths to monetization:

- Offer your services to peers and collaborators
- Request referrals from trusted contacts
- Partner for joint offers to access new audiences

A peer I collaborated with introduced me to their audience via a **joint webinar**. Within one week, I signed **5 new clients**, earning more than my usual month's revenue from a single session. Networking is not just about visibility—it's about creating **mutually beneficial opportunities that convert into income.**

Exercise:
Identify **3 key people in your network** you can collaborate with to monetize your brand this month. Outline the type of collaboration and expected results.

Step 4: Content as a Revenue Engine

Your brand content can directly lead to income:

- Use blogs, social media, or newsletters to educate and build authority
- Embed subtle calls-to-action (CTAs) for products/services
- Repurpose content across platforms to increase reach

I wrote a **10-part content series on side hustles** and embedded links to my mini-course. This campaign alone generated **₹50,000 in sales in 2 weeks** without spending a single rupee on ads. Authority plus strategic CTAs equals monetization.

Exercise:

Plan **one content series** that positions you as an expert and promotes your offer. Include at least **2 subtle CTAs** within it.

Step 5: Creating Recurring Revenue Streams

Recurring income is the key to financial freedom:

- Subscription-based services (membership communities, coaching programs)
- Retainers for ongoing services
- Digital products with automated delivery

I launched a **membership program for freelancers**, providing weekly workshops and templates. Within 3 months, it became my **largest and most predictable income stream**, giving me confidence to scale my other side hustles.

Exercise:
Brainstorm **one recurring income idea** you can implement in the next 60 days. Outline the structure, pricing, and delivery method.

Step 6: Tracking and Optimizing

To grow your monetization strategy:

- Track conversions from your network and content
- Monitor which monetization paths produce the highest ROI
- Double down on the most profitable strategies

By tracking which posts and collaborations generated the most clients, I focused my efforts on high-converting opportunities. Within 6 months, my revenue **tripled**, and I spent less time chasing low-return efforts.

Exercise:

Set up a **simple tracking sheet**: columns for monetization method, outreach, conversions, and revenue. Review weekly and adjust your strategy.

Key Takeaways

- Diversify your monetization paths to reduce risk
- Package offers to maximize perceived value
- Leverage your network strategically for new clients and collaborations
- Use content to educate, build authority, and convert
- Focus on creating recurring revenue streams for predictable income
- Track and optimize every monetization effort

Remember: **Your network and brand are not just for visibility—they are your business engine. Monetize wisely, and your side hustles can transform into sustainable wealth.**

Next Exercises:

1. List all possible ways to monetize your brand or network.
2. Draft a 3-tier offer for your primary product/service.
3. Identify 3 collaborators in your network and plan a monetization activity.
4. Create a content series with embedded CTAs for your offer.
5. Brainstorm a recurring income stream with delivery method and pricing.
6. Track conversions and optimize for maximum ROI.

56

Automating Your Hustle

"W*ork smarter, not harder.*" – Allen F. Morgenstern

Have you ever wondered why some side hustlers seem to **earn more while working less**, while you feel stuck trading hours for money? The secret is **automation**. When you automate repetitive tasks, your hustle grows **without burning you out**, freeing time for strategy, creativity, and scaling.

When I first started, I spent **6–8 hours a day manually managing clients, invoices, and emails**. I was exhausted but not growing. It wasn't until I discovered the power of automation—tools, workflows, and templates—that I could **multiply my results** without multiplying my work hours.

Step 1: Identify Repetitive Tasks

The first step in automation is **spotting what drains your time**:

- Client onboarding
- Scheduling appointments
- Social media posting
- Email follow-ups

- Invoice creation

I realized that **sending individual emails to clients and reminding them for payments** consumed almost 2 hours daily. Automating this with templates and reminders instantly freed up 10+ hours per week, which I invested in **creating new offers**.

Exercise:
List **all recurring tasks in your hustle** that consume more than 30 minutes daily. Highlight the **top 3 you can automate immediately**.

Step 2: Leverage Automation Tools

There are countless **tools designed to automate your hustle**:

- **Email automation:** MailerLite, ConvertKit, or ActiveCampaign
- **Social media scheduling:** Buffer, Later, or Hootsuite
- **Project management:** Trello, Notion, or Asana
- **Invoices & payments:** QuickBooks, PayPal, or Razorpay
- **Task automation:** Zapier, Make, or IFTTT

I integrated **Zapier with my email and CRM**, so whenever a new client signed up, they received a welcome email, invoice, and onboarding link automatically. This eliminated repetitive admin work and reduced errors.

Exercise:
Pick **2 tools** you will implement this week to automate tasks in your hustle. Write down **specific tasks each tool will handle**.

Step 3: Create Repeatable Workflows

Automation isn't just tools—it's also **structured processes**:

- Map out your workflow from lead to payment
- Identify which steps are manual
- Automate wherever possible

I created a **lead-to-client workflow**: lead capture → automated email series → consultation call → invoice → follow-up → welcome email. This system **runs on autopilot**, allowing me to handle more clients without extra effort.

Exercise:
Sketch your **main hustle workflow** in words (step-by-step). Identify at least **2 steps that can be automated**.

Step 4: Automate Content & Marketing

Content is king, but it can also be time-consuming:

- Schedule social media posts in advance
- Use email sequences to nurture leads
- Repurpose content across platforms
- Track performance automatically

I used a **content calendar and scheduling tool** to post on LinkedIn, YouTube, and Instagram without logging in daily. My email newsletter nurtured leads automatically, resulting in **5–10 new clients every month** with almost zero manual effort.

Exercise:
Plan a **1-month content calendar** and identify which parts can be **fully**

automated.

Step 5: Automate Client Communication

Communication is critical, but it can consume hours:

- Use **templates for FAQs** and common queries
- Automate follow-ups for payments, deadlines, and reminders
- Set up **chatbots** for basic customer queries

I implemented a **WhatsApp automation system** for client reminders. No more chasing payments or sending repetitive instructions. Clients loved the efficiency, and I gained more time to **focus on high-value work**.

Exercise:
Identify **3 communication tasks you perform daily**. Write down **how you can automate each task** using email, chat, or messaging tools.

Step 6: Test, Optimize, and Scale

Automation is not set-and-forget:

- Test your systems regularly
- Look for bottlenecks
- Scale what works while adjusting what doesn't

After automating my workflow, I noticed a few clients weren't receiving emails correctly. Adjusting triggers and sequences took a few hours but saved **hundreds of manual hours** in the long run. Optimization is the **secret multiplier**.

Exercise:
Set a **weekly review routine** to check your automated systems. Note 1

thing to **improve or optimize** each week.

Key Takeaways

- Identify repetitive tasks that drain your time
- Leverage tools to automate emails, content, payments, and client workflows
- Create repeatable processes that run independently
- Automate marketing, communication, and content to scale faster
- Test, optimize, and refine automation systems for maximum efficiency

Remember: **Automation is the engine that allows your side hustles to grow while you focus on strategic actions, creativity, and scaling to multiple income streams.**

Next Exercises:

1. List all repetitive tasks in your hustle and identify top 3 for immediate automation.
2. Choose 2 automation tools and map the tasks they will handle.
3. Write out your main workflow in words and mark automation opportunities.
4. Plan a 1-month content calendar and automation schedule.
5. Identify 3 communication tasks to automate.
6. Set a weekly review routine to optimize automated systems.

57

Scaling Your Network & Collaborations

"*Your network is your net worth.*" – Porter Gale

Have you ever noticed how some side hustlers seem to **always find the right opportunities, clients, or partners** while others struggle alone? The secret isn't just luck—it's **strategic networking and collaborations**. The right connections **multiply your growth**, open doors to new markets, and create income streams you never imagined.

When I first started my side hustles, I tried doing everything alone. I was grinding 12 hours a day, yet my growth was slow. Everything changed when I **actively built a network of mentors, peers, and collaborators**. Suddenly, opportunities started flowing in, joint projects increased my credibility, and I could focus on high-value tasks instead of reinventing the wheel.

Step 1: Identify Your Key Network Groups

Before you can scale your network, you need to **know who matters most**:

- **Mentors:** Experienced individuals who can guide you
- **Peers:** People hustling in the same or complementary niches

- **Clients/Customers:** Your future advocates and repeat clients
- **Collaborators:** People you can create joint projects with

I started by making a list of **10 people I admired** in my industry. I reached out to them with genuine interest, asking questions, sharing insights, and offering value. Within 6 months, I had **3 mentors and multiple peer collaborations** that accelerated my growth far beyond what I could achieve alone.

Exercise:
Write down **5–10 people** you want in each category: mentor, peer, client, collaborator. Note one actionable way to **connect with each person this month**.

Step 2: Build Relationships, Not Transactions

Networking isn't about asking for favors immediately—it's about **providing value**.

- Share knowledge freely
- Support peers and collaborators
- Celebrate others' wins
- Be consistent in communication

I reached out to a fellow freelancer offering a free **review of their marketing funnel**. That small gesture led to a **long-term collaboration** and multiple client referrals. The key was building **trust before expecting anything in return**.

Exercise:
Identify **3 people in your network** you can provide value to this week. Write down **specific ways to help them** without expecting anything in return.

Step 3: Leverage Online Platforms

Your network doesn't have to be local. Online platforms make **connecting globally** easier than ever:

- LinkedIn: Build credibility, post insights, engage in discussions
- Instagram/YouTube: Showcase your expertise and collaborate with peers
- Forums & Communities: Engage in niche-specific groups

By consistently posting actionable tips on LinkedIn, I attracted **mentorship offers, collaboration proposals, and freelance leads** from people I had never met in person.

Exercise:
Pick **2 online platforms** where your audience or peers hang out. Commit to **posting or engaging 3 times per week** this month. Track connections made.

Step 4: Initiate Collaborations

Collaboration is a **force multiplier** for side hustles:

- Joint webinars or workshops
- Co-created content or courses
- Affiliate partnerships
- Shared projects or consulting

I collaborated with a content creator who had a complementary skill set. We launched a mini-course together. The **revenue split was small**, but the **brand exposure and new clients** I gained were priceless.

Exercise:

Identify **2 potential collaborators** this month. Outline a **small project** you can do together within 30 days.

Step 5: Maintain & Nurture Your Network

Building your network is just the beginning; you need to **maintain relationships**:

- Send updates on wins, projects, or milestones
- Offer help before asking for it
- Schedule periodic check-ins
- Celebrate others' successes publicly

I make it a habit to **message 5 key contacts every week**, sharing a helpful tip or congratulating them on achievements. This simple practice keeps my network active, engaged, and ready for future collaborations.

Exercise:
Create a **weekly networking habit**. List 5 contacts you will engage with and what value you will provide.

Step 6: Track Your Growth

Just like income and side hustles, your network **requires tracking and strategy**:

- Track collaborations and their outcomes
- Monitor new leads or opportunities from your network
- Evaluate what types of connections provide the **highest growth potential**

I maintained a simple document tracking **every collaboration, lead, and referral**. This helped me **double my side hustle revenue in 6 months** just by focusing on the right relationships.

Exercise:

Start a **Network Tracker** in a notebook or spreadsheet. Record each new connection, engagement, and outcome. Review monthly for opportunities to improve.

Key Takeaways

- Focus on mentors, peers, clients, and collaborators
- Build relationships by **providing value first**
- Leverage online platforms to scale your reach
- Initiate small, mutually beneficial collaborations
- Maintain, nurture, and track your network regularly
- Treat your network as a **growth engine**, not just contacts

Remember: **A strong network multiplied with automation and scalable side hustles is the formula for building financial freedom faster than going it alone.**

Next Exercises:

1. List 5–10 key people in each network category: mentors, peers, clients, collaborators.
2. Offer value to 3 people this week without expecting anything in return.
3. Commit to 2 online platforms for engagement and posting.
4. Identify 2 potential collaborations and outline a mini-project.
5. Set up a weekly habit to nurture your top 5 connections.
6. Start a network tracker to measure growth and outcomes.

58

Monetizing Your Brand & Network

"Your network isn't just for connections—it's a goldmine waiting to be activated."

Have you ever wondered why some side hustlers seem to **effortlessly turn contacts into clients, collaborations into revenue, and influence into income**? The secret isn't just working hard—it's **strategically monetizing your brand and network**.

When I first realized the power of my network, I had hundreds of connections but **no system to leverage them**. One small change—**treating relationships as opportunities to provide value while creating mutual benefit**—transformed my side hustles into sustainable income streams. Suddenly, my collaborations were generating consistent revenue, and my personal brand attracted new clients without cold outreach.

Step 1: Identify Monetizable Relationships

Not every connection will generate revenue, but **some relationships can unlock high-value opportunities**:

- Collaborators for joint projects

- Mentors who can introduce you to high-ticket clients
- Peers who can exchange leads
- Audience members or followers ready to invest

I had a mentor who connected me to a client willing to pay **₹50,000 for a consulting session**. That single introduction more than doubled my side hustle revenue that month.

Exercise:
List **5 people in your network** who could become clients, collaborators, or referral partners. Note **one actionable step to approach each** this month.

Step 2: Offer High-Value Solutions

Monetization requires **packaging your expertise** in a way people are willing to pay for:

- Small digital products (templates, guides, mini-courses)
- Services (freelancing, consulting, coaching)
- Joint ventures (webinars, co-branded products)

I created a **mini-course priced at ₹999** for beginners in my niche. By leveraging my existing network and past collaborators for promotion, I sold **over 200 copies in the first month**.

Exercise:
Identify **one high-value product or service** you can offer this month to your network. Write down **3 ways to market it** through existing connections.

Step 3: Turn Followers into Customers

Your personal brand and content create trust. Monetization happens when you **guide your audience from free value to paid solutions**:

- Share helpful tips, stories, and case studies
- Introduce your paid services naturally
- Highlight results and testimonials from early clients

I shared a personal story on LinkedIn about **how I scaled a side hustle to ₹10,000/month**. The post received engagement, and several connections signed up for my consulting services—without me sending a single direct sales message.

Exercise:

Draft **one story-driven post** showcasing a small win or result. Include a subtle call-to-action for your product or service.

Step 4: Collaborations as Revenue Streams

Monetizing your network isn't just about selling; it's about **creating mutually beneficial partnerships**:

- Co-create a product with a peer
- Launch a joint webinar with a collaborator
- Exchange services or cross-promote

I collaborated with another freelancer to host a **webinar on building digital side hustles**. Our combined audiences paid ₹499 each, and we split the revenue while gaining **long-term email subscribers and repeat clients**.

Exercise:

Identify **2 collaborators** and brainstorm a small project or offer you can launch together within 30 days.

Step 5: Track and Optimize Revenue

Just like a side hustle, monetizing your network **requires measurement and optimization**:

- Track which collaborations generate the highest revenue
- Measure engagement vs. conversion
- Refine offers and messaging for maximum impact

By tracking the **source of each client and collaboration**, I realized that LinkedIn connections and past collaborators generated **3x more revenue than cold outreach**. I shifted focus accordingly, doubling my income in 90 days.

Exercise:

Create a **Revenue Tracker**: List all income sources from your network, note the type (collaboration, client, affiliate, product), and measure revenue monthly.

Key Takeaways

- Focus on **high-value relationships** that can generate revenue
- Offer solutions your network is willing to pay for
- Use your personal brand to **convert followers into customers**
- Collaborate strategically for mutual benefit and increased reach
- Track results and optimize continuously

Remember: **Your network, when properly leveraged, can become a consistent and scalable revenue engine—turning side hustles into sustainable wealth and financial freedom.**

Next Exercises:

1. List 5 connections in your network to monetize this month.
2. Identify one high-value service, product, or offer to market.
3. Draft a story-driven post guiding followers toward your offer.
4. Plan 2 collaboration projects with peers or mentors.
5. Set up a monthly revenue tracker to monitor network monetization.

59

Automating Your Hustle

"Work smarter, not harder. Systems turn effort into consistent results."

Have you ever felt like no matter how much you hustle, **there aren't enough hours in the day** to grow your side business? The truth is, **manual effort alone caps your income and freedom.** Automation allows you to **scale your side hustles while freeing up time**, so you can focus on growth, creativity, and high-value tasks.

When I first started, I spent hours manually sending emails, posting content, and managing clients. It was exhausting. Once I implemented simple systems—**automated email follow-ups, scheduling tools, and workflow templates**—my productivity skyrocketed, and my revenue started growing even when I wasn't actively working.

Step 1: Identify Repetitive Tasks

Automation begins with **spotting tasks that repeat daily or weekly**:

- Email follow-ups
- Social media posting
- Client onboarding

- Content repurposing

I realized I was **spending 3–4 hours per week manually sending follow-ups** to potential clients. Once I set up an automated email sequence, the same clients were contacted automatically, saving me 12–16 hours per month—time I used to create new products and grow my network.

Exercise:
Make a list of **all repetitive tasks in your side hustle**. Highlight **3 tasks you could automate this month**.

Step 2: Choose Simple Tools

Automation doesn't have to be complex or expensive. For beginners:

- **Email Automation:** MailerLite, ConvertKit, or free Gmail templates
- **Social Media Scheduling:** Buffer, Canva Scheduler, or Later
- **Project & Workflow Management:** Trello, Notion, Asana
- **Payment & Invoicing:** PayPal, Stripe, Razorpay

I started with **free versions of MailerLite and Trello**. Even with minimal investment, I **saved 8–10 hours per week** and avoided missed follow-ups that could have cost me clients.

Exercise:
Pick **2 tools from the list above** and implement them this week. Track the time saved.

Step 3: Automate Client Onboarding

Every client or customer experience should be **smooth, consistent, and mostly automated**:

- Create a **welcome email sequence**
- Share instructions, deliverables, and payment links automatically
- Include FAQs and support resources

I created an **automated onboarding email sequence** for my consulting clients. Instead of spending an hour per client explaining processes, clients now receive all details automatically. This allowed me to **handle more clients without extra effort**.

Exercise:
Draft a **3-step onboarding email sequence** for your clients or customers this month.

Step 4: Repurpose & Automate Content

Content fuels your brand and network, but creating everything manually is unsustainable:

- Repurpose blog posts into videos, social media snippets, and email newsletters
- Use scheduling tools to **publish consistently without daily effort**

I took one LinkedIn article, turned it into **5 short posts, 1 video, and an email newsletter**, and scheduled them for the month. The same content generated **leads and engagement** while I focused on other revenue-generating tasks.

Exercise:

Choose **one piece of content** this week and plan **3 ways to repurpose it**. Schedule it using a tool.

Step 5: Automate Follow-Ups & Sales Funnels

Your network and audience can be monetized more efficiently with **simple sales funnels and follow-up systems**:

- Free lead magnet → Email sequence → Paid offer
- Reminder emails for abandoned carts or unclaimed offers
- Upsell or cross-sell follow-ups

I set up a **simple lead magnet funnel** for my side hustle. Leads who opted in automatically received **3 value-packed emails** before being presented with my paid course. Within a month, it generated **₹30,000+ in sales** without me manually messaging anyone.

Exercise:

Draft a **mini funnel for one of your products or services**: Lead magnet → 3 emails → paid offer.

Key Takeaways

- Identify repetitive tasks and focus on automating them first
- Use simple, beginner-friendly tools to save time
- Automate client onboarding, follow-ups, and content distribution
- Repurpose content to maximize reach without extra effort
- Use sales funnels to convert leads and network into consistent revenue

Remember: **Automation doesn't replace your creativity—it multiplies it. By systematizing repetitive work, you free your time to grow, innovate, and scale your side hustles toward real financial freedom.**

Next Exercises:

1. List 3 tasks to automate this month.
2. Pick 2 tools and implement automation.
3. Create a 3-step client onboarding sequence.
4. Repurpose one content piece into 3 formats.
5. Draft a mini funnel for a product or service.

60

Your Personal Action Plan & Next Steps

"A *goal without a plan is just a wish." – Antoine de Saint-Exupéry*

You've learned mindset shifts, side hustle strategies, brand-building, automation, and network growth. But all of this knowledge **only becomes powerful when you take action**. Are you ready to **turn your learning into results** and finally break free from the middle-class trap?

When I first started my journey, I felt overwhelmed. There were so many ideas, tools, and strategies that I didn't know where to begin. The solution was simple: **create a step-by-step action plan with small, measurable milestones**. Today, that same approach has helped me scale multiple income streams, automate workflows, and build sustainable financial freedom.

Step 1: Set Your 6-Month Goals

Your goals should be **specific, measurable, and realistic**, yet ambitious enough to push you out of your comfort zone.

- Revenue targets: e.g., first ₹10k, ₹50k, ₹1 lakh
- Skill development: e.g., mastering content creation, freelancing platforms, or sales
- Network growth: connect with 10 mentors or collaborators

Exercise:

Write down **3 key goals for the next 6 months**. Include revenue, skills, and network targets.

Step 2: Break Goals into Monthly Milestones

Small wins build confidence and momentum. Divide your 6-month goals into **actionable monthly steps**:

- Month 1: Identify side hustle, choose tools, create first offer
- Month 2: Launch first product/service, gather feedback
- Month 3: Build email list, automate 1 task
- Month 4: Scale content, network, and collaborations
- Month 5: Refine automation, upsell or cross-sell offers
- Month 6: Review, measure, and plan for next 6 months

Exercise:

Create a **monthly milestone table** in paragraph form: write each month's main focus and 2–3 tasks you will accomplish.

Step 3: Daily & Weekly Action Steps

Consistency is key. Create **daily and weekly routines** that align with your milestones:

- Daily: 1 hour on skill development, 1 hour on side hustle

- Weekly: 1 networking session, 1 content piece, 1 automated task implemented

Exercise:

Write a **weekly action checklist**: what you will do every week for the next month to achieve your milestones.

Step 4: Build Accountability

Even the best plan can fail without accountability. Options include:

- Sharing your goals with a friend or mentor
- Joining a community or mastermind
- Tracking progress publicly in a journal or social media (optional)

When I started, I **shared my 30-day goals with a mentor**. This simple act kept me consistent and motivated, and I **achieved revenue targets faster than I imagined**.

Exercise:

Choose **one accountability method** and set it up this week.

Step 5: Review, Reflect, and Reinvest

Every month, **review your progress**:

- What worked?
- What didn't work?
- Which tasks can be automated or delegated?
- How can you reinvest earnings into your growth?

Exercise:

Write a **monthly reflection**: 3 things you learned, 2 things to improve, and 1 way to reinvest your earnings.

Step 6: Plan for Scaling

Once your first income streams are stable, think about **next-level growth**:

- Multiple side hustles
- Productized services
- Affiliate marketing and collaborations
- Automating further to free your time

After implementing small, consistent steps, I **scaled from earning ₹10k/-month to multiple revenue streams generating ₹1 lakh+ monthly**. Automation, smart networking, and reinvesting made it possible.

Exercise:

Write down **2 new ways to scale your side hustles** over the next 6 months.

Key Takeaways

- Action beats knowledge—implement step-by-step
- Break 6-month goals into monthly, weekly, and daily tasks
- Use accountability to stay consistent
- Reflect and reinvest consistently
- Always plan for scaling and automation

Remember: **A side hustle isn't just a way to earn—it's your bridge to financial freedom. By following this action plan, you're taking**

control of your time, income, and future. Start small, stay consistent, and think big. Your freedom is waiting.

61

Invitation

Congratulations! You now have the roadmap to **shift your mindset and start building wealth**. If you're ready to **accelerate your journey**, I've created a complete online course that:

- Provides **step-by-step guidance** to start and scale your side hustle.
- Shares **templates, worksheets, and action plans** for beginners.
- Offers a **community of like-minded learners** for support and accountability.
- Includes **case studies and strategies** to fast-track your first ₹10k, ₹50k, and beyond.

Take the next step:

"Ready to take the next step? Explore my online courses, join live webinars, and access exclusive templates and blueprints to accelerate your journey from knowledge to real digital income. Visit www.takshaydigitalacademy.com *and start building your digital empire today!"*

Visit to join our courses

Join now and turn your side hustle into **real financial freedom**.

Series Companion Map – "Digital Wealth Ecosystem"

Here's how Book 12 fits into the **full 12-book ecosystem** and funnels you to courses and actionable income:

Step 1 – Mindset & Foundation

- Book 1: Digital Coach Blueprint
- Book 2: 10X Digital Coach Mastery
- Book 3: 10X Funnel Mindset Secrets

Step 2 – Ads, Funnels, and Business Skills

- Book 4: Meta Ads Secrets
- Book 5: Google Ads Secrets
- Book 6: Digital Empire

Step 3 – Financial Mindset & Side Hustle Growth

- Book 7: Rock Bottom to Digital Freedom
- Book 8: Middle-Class Trap to Millionaire Mindset
- Book 9: Side Hustle to Financial Freedom

Step 4 – AI & Social Media Mastery

- Book 10: Decode YouTube Algorithm
- Book 11: Decode Instagram Algorithm
- Book 12: The AI Millionaire

Step 5 – Courses & Live Coaching

- Use these books as your **roadmap to digital freedom**
- Each book includes exercises, worksheets, and companion resources
- Join courses and webinars to scale faster and automate income

62

Lets Connect / Join Our Community

Let's Stay Connected

AUTHOR :- TARUN TAKSHAY

The author would like to interact with you and receive your feedback. Get in touch and send him your reviews

www.takshaydigitalacademy.com
www.taruntakshay.com
tarun@taruntakshay.com
www.youtube.com/digitaltakshay
www.instagram.com/taruntakshay
www.facebook.com/taruntakshay
https://www.linkedin.com/in/tarun-takshay/
https://digitaltakshay.com/

Thank you !

This book may end here, but our journey together doesn't have to. I'd love to hear your story—what resonated with you, what breakthroughs you experienced, and how you're applying these systems in your coaching business.

📧 You can reach me directly at: **info@takshaydigitalacademy.com**
🌐 Or visit my website: https://www.takshaydigitalacademy.com/

You can also connect with me on social media to get updates, free resources, and ongoing mentorship. Just search for "**Tarun Takshay**" and join the community.

63

Conclusion

Your Journey Begins Now

"The path to financial freedom isn't a straight line—it's a series of small, intentional steps. What matters is that you start today."

By now, you've learned:

- How to **shift your mindset** from employee to owner.
- Why **taking calculated risks** accelerates growth.
- How **side hustles** can become sustainable income streams.
- The importance of **time management, reinvestment, and habits**.
- How to **avoid common traps** that keep middle-class earners stuck.

Key Reminder: Financial independence is not an abstract goal. Every hour you invest, every rupee you reinvest, and every small win compounds toward **real freedom and wealth**.

Action: Pick one small step from this book and do it **within the next 24 hours**. Momentum starts with action.

Epilogue

As you turn the final pages of this book, I want you to pause for a moment and reflect.

You began this journey with a simple question: *"Is there more to life than the routine of work, bills, and limited choices?"*

Now, you know the answer. Yes — there is more. Much more.

The truth is, the **middle-class trap** was never about money alone. It was about mindset. It was about believing that security comes only from a paycheck, that success is measured only by titles and possessions, and that life must always be lived within boundaries someone else sets for you.

But you've seen that the moment you shift your thinking, everything changes. You start seeing opportunities instead of obstacles. You start making choices based on growth, not fear. You start living life on your terms.

Becoming a millionaire — in wealth, in mindset, in freedom — is not an event. It's a journey. It's a series of daily decisions, small shifts, and consistent actions that compound over time. And here's the most powerful truth: *you already have everything within you to begin.*

Don't wait for the "perfect time." Don't wait for permission. Don't wait for certainty. Start now, with what you have, where you are.

One day, you'll look back and realize that the greatest investment you ever made wasn't in stocks, real estate, or business. It was in yourself — in your growth, your mindset, and your belief that you were capable of so much more.

This book may end here, but your journey is only beginning.

The middle-class trap is behind you. The millionaire mindset is in front of you. The choice, as always, is yours.

You've reached the final pages of this book, but in truth — this is the first page of your new life.

The middle-class trap whispers: *"Go back to comfort. Don't change. Stay safe."* But deep inside, you know that comfort is the enemy of growth. Comfort will never give you freedom.

The millionaire mindset shouts: *"Break free. Take action. Trust yourself. Build the life you deserve."*

Every single person who ever achieved greatness stood where you stand now — at the crossroads between old thinking and new possibilities. Some turned back. But the ones who pressed forward? They became the success stories we admire today.

So I'll ask you: **Which one will you be?**

Your journey doesn't end with closing this book. It begins here. The mindset is yours now. The tools are yours. The question is — will you act on them?

Take one bold step today. Invest in yourself. Challenge your limits. Apply what you've learned, and when fear whispers, remind yourself: *"I am no longer trapped. I am unstoppable."*

And if you're ready to go even deeper, I've created a proven system to walk you step by step into this new life. Join me, and let's make your millionaire mindset a living reality.

The trap is broken. The path is open.
Your future is waiting.
And it belongs to you.

Tarun Takshay

Afterword

Dear Reader,

Writing this book has been a personal journey. I know what it feels like to be trapped in the routine of a 9–5, dreaming of financial freedom but unsure how to start. Every story, exercise, and strategy here comes from **my own experience** building side hustles, learning from failures, and gradually moving toward financial independence.

My goal is simple: to **help you break free from comfort, fear, and doubt**—and start building your own wealth, one small step at a time.

I hope this book becomes your **companion, guide, and motivator** as you take the journey from middle-class mindset to millionaire mindset.

As you put this book down, I want you to remember one thing: **you are far more powerful than you've ever been told.**

The middle-class trap is not your destiny — it's just a temporary stop. The fears, the doubts, the limitations you once carried are not permanent. They are nothing more than stories you've been repeating to yourself. And stories can be rewritten.

You now hold the pen. You get to write the next chapter of your life.

Never again say, *"I can't."* Instead, ask, *"How can I?"*

Never again wait for the perfect time. Instead, declare, *"Now is my time."*

Never again see yourself as average. Instead, remind yourself, *"I am limitless."*

The world doesn't change when you wait. It changes when you act. And you — right here, right now — are ready to act.

Let this book be the line in the sand where you said: *"Enough is enough. I will no longer live small. I choose growth. I choose freedom. I choose the millionaire mindset."*

Your dreams are not too big. They are exactly the size they need to be to stretch you, to grow you, and to remind you of what's possible.

So step forward. Take action. Believe in yourself even when no one else does. And remember — the greatest wealth you will ever build is not measured in money, but in the freedom, confidence, and courage to live life on your terms.

This is your afterword. But it's also your new beginning.

Go out there and prove to yourself what I already know: **you were never meant to stay trapped. You were born to be free.**

Author -
Tarun Takshay

www.ingramcontent.com/pod-product-compliance
Ingram Content Group UK Ltd.
Pitfield, Milton Keynes, MK11 3LW, UK
UKHW021404190726
13845UKWH00028B/869

9 789334 442762